Unapologetically ENOUGH

RESHAPING SUCCESS AND SELF-LOVE

CARRIE SEVERSON

Unapologetically Enough

© 2022. Carrie Severson. All rights reserved.

Published in the United States by the Unapologetic Voice House. The Unapologetic Voice House is a hybrid publishing house focused on publishing strong female voices and stories.

www.theunapologeticvoicehouse.com

Paperback ISBN: 978-1-955090-03-2
E-book ISBN: 978-1-955090-11-7

Library of Congress Control Number: 2021909010

Gavin,

I'm so grateful our roads finally crossed. Life is better with you beside me. I look forward to experiencing all God has planned for us.

I love you.

Unapologetically.

There's no road map to life.

Only soul quests filled with self-discovery, growth, acceptance, love, purpose, fear, struggle, suffocation, balance, stories, truth, change, spirituality, and lots of surprises.

It takes a lot of guts and effort to truly see ourselves as unapologetically enough.

And it's all worth it.

Contents

Preface

IT TOOK TWENTY-EIGHT YEARS FOR ME TO UNCOVER THE FACT that I'm an empath. That's probably my favorite trait about myself. I'm also a lover, warrior, spiritual truth seeker, soul sister, storyteller, recovered burnout, fertility experiment, and hopeful romantic with endless optimism for mankind. I'm also unapologetically enough of all those things.

Even though I've been on a road of deep self-discovery for more than twenty years, I didn't really wake up until I decided it was time to go on a soul quest in search of my voice—my true voice, my unapologetic voice.

That soul quest started on my thirty-fifth birthday. And it lasted the next eight years.

My journey to accepting myself as a remarkable, unapologetic, divine, loving woman included a dozen coaches, a variety of yoga techniques, all kinds of meditation practices, a self-induced burnout, three businesses, countless dating-profiles, and two fertility experiments that broke my heart and put me through an intense immune system reboot. I encountered two big parts of myself while resting and recovering in my hometown of Menomonee Falls, Wisconsin. It was a safe place for me to recoup. During my first extended recovery stint, my childhood home was still without internet access or cell phone reception. If I really wanted to make a phone call on my cell, I had to stand in one specific spot in the street.

I eased my way back into real life after that first summer of recovery. I spent the next year of my life seeking out happiness. Eventually, I wrote a blog post called "I'm A Recovering Burnout" for the Huffington Post. That post and the response I received after it was what sparked the inspiration to write this book. Women from all around the world reached out to me to thank me for my vulnerability and my strength. I had a woman e-mail me from Ireland who wanted advice on how to start a nonprofit to get prostitutes off the streets, and one man in Australia even quit his job after reading my blog. He took his savings and went on a six-month walkabout. Everyone encouraged me to keep writing, keep sharing my story.

I was invited to write for more platforms after that piece gained attention. What I realized was that people wanted to learn how to recover from their own burnout. They wanted to learn how to take a leap of faith. They wanted to address issues in their own lives, not just hear what I did to change mine.

After my recovery from my burnout, I was able to open my heart again. I found myself on a really bad date one night with a man who told me I had missed my chance to get married and have kids. That experience wound up as an essay called "I'm 37, Not A Missed Opportunity" and landed in a women's magazine.

The response from that essay helped me understand the importance of writing this book.

It also led me to take a deep look at my love life. I dated many amazing men in my twenties and thirties but didn't find the one I wanted to spend forever with. So I created a contract with myself and promised myself that if I didn't meet the man I wanted to build a life with by the time I was thirty-eight, I would take action to preserve my fertility.

He didn't show.

So I found a doctor.

After two rounds of fertility treatments, I had ruined my immune system. I spent the majority of my next year in and out of doctors' offices or sick in bed, rebuilding my immune system from scratch. Between my burnout recovery and my immune system reboot, I had time to fall more deeply in love with myself. It took all my effort and energy—I was dedicated to it—but I did it.

This book is my self-discovery. It's my awakening journey. It's how I finally saw and met myself. It's how I came back to me. Or maybe how I met myself for the first time. Either way, this is a record of a few different soul quests.

It took me eight years to complete this book and put it out into the world.

And the title of this beautiful piece changed six times. I won't share the other five titles in the event that I actually want to use those someday.

It was my editor, Danielle, who brought the title, *Unapologetically Enough*, to my attention.

The word *enough* was a trigger word for me for a long time, so when she gave me her opinion for the title of this book, *Unapologetically Enough*, I clenched my jaw and disengaged from her e-mail. I immediately sent a text to a spiritual coach of mine.

"My editor thinks the book is called *Unapologetically Enough*."

"I like it. How does your heart feel with it?"

"My heart is racing. I can feel some kinda energy brewing up within me, and I think I'm about to cry and maybe vomit," I said.

My coach said, "Look up synonyms." And then she sent the angel emoji.

I typed the words *enough* and *synonym* in my search engine and felt a surge of emotion swell in my chest when I saw *abundant* and *full*.

It wasn't until Danielle suggested the title that I realized I never addressed why the word was a trigger for me.

So after an hour or so, I sat down and leaned into it. And tears came. And came. And came. And the more I dug into it, the better I felt. The more excited I felt, too. Tears turned into fits of laughter. I landed right in the middle of something I had to call my own.

The word *enough* was a trigger for me because during my burnout recovery I was able to see that I overused the word in a negative fashion. Rather than turn to it and pull it toward me as a way to heal that deep wound, I pushed it away. I locked that idea of not having enough, not being enough, not doing enough, being sick and tired of being sick and tired in a closet.

4

Finally, in the last year of working on this book I embraced *enough*. I claimed it. I declared it. I became it. I am it. Unapologetically. Boldly. Fiercely. Femininely. Wildly.

I love what we're capable of doing with our lives once we tell ourselves we can. More than that, though, I love who we are able to grow into once we give ourselves permission to believe it.

If you're currently lost, I hope this book finds you and helps you map out your own soul quest. I am where I am today because I chased the void. It took a long time, but my void is gone. I lost the need to look for it, feel it, and fill it.

And trust me, my friend, if the word *enough* is a trigger for you, I know what you're going through. Keep on moving. I promise you it gets better. You have to do the work. Feel the fire, face the pain, and let it remold you. You'll be so grateful for the experience once you're on the other side.

My hope is that you will not be the same person when you get to the end of this book as the one you are today.

Read this with time. And some grace. I've also included journaling entries throughout the book because I'm a long-time journaling junkie and they hold a special power for me. It's how I've gone inward, opened up my heart, surrendered, and healed. I had boxes and boxes of journals dating back decades in my garage when I wrote this book for the last time. I held on to those pages when I was at my rock bottom, and I celebrated myself when I was at the top. My journaling experience might be different from yours, and that's just fine. You do you.

There are exercises in the back of the book that I used over the course of my journey to help me recognize my own divine magnetism. There are journal prompts there, too. Use what you find helpful and leave the rest. Maybe come back to it another time. We are all on a unique journey. Honor yours.

I hope you enjoy this. I think you will. Call me if you don't. Or maybe e-mail. E-mail's better. Yeah. E-mail me.

I love you.

Unapologetically.

Part I

AN UNAPOLOGETIC VOICE ON SUCCESS

Chapter One

FIGHT-OR-FLIGHT

I'VE ALWAYS KNOWN I WAS DIFFERENT. I GREW FASTER THAN any other kid in school and peaked at five foot nine when I was ten years old. I was known as "the big guy in the middle" whenever I was forced to play basketball because I was, well, taller than anyone else playing.

I was bullied more than other girls. I laughed louder. I cried more. I weighed more. In general, I *was* more. And many times I was told I was too much of one thing or another. The fact was, I was a sponge. I consumed other people's emotions until they felt like my own. I just didn't know that at the time.

As a creative person, the ability to feel deeply has been a blessing as often as it's been a curse. My true calling in life is to communicate in a raw, real fashion. I grew up onstage as a dancer and loved the spotlight. But in college, my form of expression turned to story-telling. Using my extra helping of emotions and feelings has been a big factor in accepting myself and finding my voice.

I have the soul of someone who experienced the seventies. Unfortunately, I'm actually a product of the eighties. And the eighties were pretty rough for an overweight, self-conscious empath . . .

It was difficult to find someone who looked like me portrayed in the media throughout my childhood. I would seek approval from my peers and not find it, so I would always end up consoling myself with food. Then I'd punish myself for overeating. That was my cycle from the time I was eight till I was eighteen.

As a result of being mistreated by my peers, I had a lot of trouble connecting to others and an even harder time loving myself. What others said about me and my body became my identity, and no matter how much I covered my body, after a while, all I saw was what they saw. Identifying myself as a fat girl wasn't just an evil I endured; it became a punishment I gave myself. I accepted that identity as my fate. I couldn't escape it. I convinced myself that I was unworthy of healthy relationships. My self-esteem worsened because of it, which made me an even greater target for bullying throughout middle school.

One morning in seventh grade, I woke my parents up before the bus came to take me to school. I told them I wanted to stay home because there was a group of girls who were going to beat me up. My parents reassured me that I'd be fine. They didn't know this group of girls, though. There was no way I was going to be fine. These girls were flat-out mean, batshit crazy girls.

The teachers even avoided the leader of this particular pack. Nobody really knew anything about her family; she did just enough work to get by each class and was typically in detention.

"Please let me stay home, Mom."

"It'll be fine."

While still lying in bed, my dad showed me how to throw a left hook and an uppercut just to be on the safe side.

My fight-or-flight instinct kicked into high gear that morning before school.

I walked back into my bedroom and paced in front of my dresser. Out of nowhere, an idea came to me. I ripped open one of my drawers and fumbled through it until I saw a big, black, chunky beaded bracelet. It was a costume bracelet I got from my great-aunt, but I never wore it. I wrapped it in tissue paper, put it in my backpack, and then went off to the bus. On the ride to school that morning, I worked out a plan in my head. I decided to use the bracelet as a payment of sorts in exchange for protection.

The girl I decided to ask for help was the toughest kid in school. She wore black makeup and a black leather jacket every day. She dated a high school kid and smoked cigarettes. We were nothing alike. For some reason, though, she liked me. She liked my laugh. She liked the fact that my eyes were gray. She liked my crazy curly hair. And I think she felt a little sorry for me.

I was going to use all that to my advantage.

When I got to school, I waited by her locker. As soon as I saw her strutting down the hallway, I took the bracelet out of my backpack. I got ready. I planted my feet firmly on the floor and took a deep breath. I smiled at her and spun the bracelet around my fingers.

Her eyes locked on the clunky jewelry as I told her my problem. I handed her the bracelet, and I promised that if she made sure I didn't get beat up, I'd continue to bring her jewelry like that. She screamed and jumped up and down. I laughed with relief. It was as though I had my own personal fairy godmother, even if she didn't look like the fairies portrayed in cartoons. And already had a smoker's cough. But none of that really mattered to me.

A month later, my mom and I went shopping, and I picked out these big, black, dangly crucifix earrings for my second installment. Back then, crucifix jewelry represented heavy metal more than it did faith, and thanks to my heavy metal guardian angel, I got through seventh grade without getting beat up.

I was a businesswoman even then. I just didn't know it or have the confidence to embrace it. I would have made an awesome lemonade-stand entrepreneur, though, I'm sure.

My imagination was a savior throughout my childhood. It was vivid and fluid, and my creative landscape of make-believe was massive. Writing was great therapy for me, and when I wanted to curl up and cry because of things kids would say to me or how I felt at the end of the day, I always came home to write.

Writing and dancing were my first true loves. They still are. Even though I was ashamed of my body and my weight, I thrived in the dance studio and loved being onstage. I would bind my body up so tight I couldn't really breathe, which is a problem for an overweight dancer.

I'd gotten that brilliant idea when I was sixteen years old. I decided to wrap my torso in two ACE bandages so the audience would believe I was thinner. I didn't want them to really see me. Or see too much of me.

As a young girl who didn't feel like she was enough, my fight-or-flight instinct was to run as far as I could and fight anyone who got in the way. So when the start of my senior year of high school hit, I applied to two colleges. One was a small school in upstate Wisconsin that had 1,300 students. The other was Arizona State University, where there were 35,000 students. I got into both. I wanted so bad to move to the other side of the country and start my life. I was over being a girl who lacked self-esteem and who lived more freely in her make-believe world than she did in her real one.

But my parents weren't ready for me to live on the other side of the country at eighteen so I spent my first year of college in upstate Wisconsin.

Luckily, the tiny school I went to had a coed boxing club. I hit a bag every day and released all the pent-up anger I had carried around with me, trapped in the cells of my body, for ten years. It worked, too. It may not have been the best therapy in terms of truly dealing with my feelings, but it felt good. *I* felt good. Plus, I lost eighty pounds that year!

As much as I enjoyed my initial transformation, I outgrew the school quickly. I was ready to explore something more. I wanted something bigger. I wanted to experience life in a way I couldn't in small-town Wisconsin. I was ready to go.

I transferred to Arizona State University my sophomore year of college and graduated with a degree in journalism in 2000. My big dream was to get a job at a magazine, become the editor-in-chief of that magazine, and then change where the spotlight landed. I figured if magazines were sharing stories about "real people" instead of supermodels and celebrities, women would have a wider variety of role models to look up to. And they would stop being so hard on themselves and they'd raise girls who would learn how not to be shitty to other girls.

My first job out of college was writing for a magazine that covered promotional products. I wrote about hats and water bottle labels and anything else that had a logo on it. I was once charged with writing twenty-five hundred words about *pens*. And it was actually really hard! What comes after "It writes in blue ink"? Seriously, what do you say after that? Thankfully, this was before Google, so you won't be able to find that piece even if you tried. I already searched. Don't bother. You can't find it.

But at least I was writing. To this day, my friends never let me forget that my first real writing gig post-college was for a magazine that reported on pens.

I wrote throughout the majority of my twenties. In the back of my mind, I knew I wanted to change the way girls treated other girls and women treated other women. I just had a lot of life to live first.

By the time I turned twenty-five, I recognized I had to really deal with my unhealthy fight-or-flight instinct. The way I handled stress had created a void in my life. It felt like a weight on my chest constricting my breath from fully escaping, and it never eased up to allow any more breath to sneak in. Since I didn't know how to change society for the better at that point in my life, I spent thousands of dollars looking for ways to simply fill the void.

I affectionately call my late twenties "my exploration phase."

First, I set out on a mission to find new hobbies, join new clubs, and create a new identity. When I'd sink my hooks into something new, I didn't just jump on the bandwagon, I became the *captain* for the bandwagon.

I made a deal with myself during those years: I would try anything once. And if I loved it, I'd continue exploring it and let whatever was supposed to unfold, well, unfold. If it felt too outside my comfort zone, I'd usually leave whatever class or adventure I was on without looking back.

I hoped that a new hobby would spark something deep within my soul and lead me to fulfilling my life's purpose. But I had no idea what I was looking for.

I started this phase of my life in the most logical place I could think of: the bookstore. In fact, I visited a new bookstore every weekend. I stood in the aisles on Saturday afternoons, staring at the colorful covers. I stood there waiting for something—*any-thing*—to catch my eye. I was most attracted to DIY, hobby, travel, and biography books.

To sum up my exploration phase, here is a list of hobbies I picked up between the ages of twenty-two and twenty-nine:

- Horseback riding
- Painting
- Nonfiction writing
- Scrapbooking
- Feng shui
- Event planning
- Interior design
- A raw-food diet
- Hot yoga

I would move on to a new hobby when I realized I wasn't any good at the current hobby. In the case of horseback riding, I pretty much stopped after a horse named Bubba threw me into a tree and knocked me unconscious. Bubba and I broke up immediately. I haven't trusted anyone named Bubba since. I know, I know. I have to do some therapy work around this later. It's on my to-do list.

Painting also didn't go very well. My artistic talent hadn't improved since I was ten, and everyone knew I had no business taking an art class. All I did was paint hearts and flowers. I dropped the class after a few sessions and enrolled in a creative-writing class.

I thought I'd be a natural at fiction writing. Words are my superpower, after all. But it turns out that, nope, I'm not all that good at writing make-believe.

I still scrapbook and love decorating. Now I pay people to come into my home and move things around according to feng shui principles. Event planning is my sister's thing. For me, it's just plain stressful, and I'm more of a Pilates lady than a yoga lady. I tried all kinds of yoga, too. And eating raw food just made me bloated and gassy.

Even though I didn't find what I was looking for in any of the hobbies I explored during my twenties, every one of those attempts introduced me to new people and gave me some beautiful moments.

In February 2008, six months before my thirtieth birthday, a friend of mine asked me if I was looking for a *spiritual* awakening in my yoga class.

"I'm searching for answers to my life so, yeah, I guess I'm here for a spiritual awakening," I said.

That one simple conversation stayed with me the entire day. I ended up back at a bookstore. I walked up to the girl behind the customer service counter and asked, "Where would I go to learn about spirituality?"

"Are you looking for a specific book?" she asked.

"Well, I don't know anything about the topic, really, so I just wanted to explore," I said.

She raised her eyebrows at me and gave me a crooked smile. "New Age."

The New Age section was filled with concepts and titles I had never heard of before. I tossed my purse in the corner and plopped down on the floor. I stayed there for hours. I skimmed dozens of books. My quest to understand my own spirituality became *an obsession.*

Chapter Two

ANGEL ANGIE

IT WAS A SATURDAY AFTERNOON IN EARLY FEBRUARY 2008. MY weekend started out like most. I met my Pilates instructor for a session at her studio, then walked over to my favorite weekend coffee shop for a hazelnut coffee before driving over to my little corner market. I grabbed a basket and filled it with berries, eggs, and BBQ chicken. Then I piled on goodies and snacks I only treated myself to on Saturdays. Flavored chips. Bagels. Something with chocolate in it. A frozen pizza. I stood in the frozen aisle and took a quick guilt trip. I traded out the deep-dish pizza for a gluten-free, dairy-free pizza. It was twice as expensive.

I charged the groceries and went home. I unpacked everything, toasted a bagel, slathered butter on it, ate it, and showered as quickly as possible. I rushed over to the nail salon for a mani-pedi appointment. I was in a red mood in 2008, and my nails and toes had to match, so I grabbed two different shades of red and selected the one with a better name.

Afterward, I drove across town for my monthly eyebrow-shaping appointment with Amy.

"So what's new?" she asked as she laid hot wax around my eyes.

"I was at the bookstore last week and found this book about the Law of Attraction," I said. "It's really cool."

"I can't believe you just said that," Amy screamed.

I opened my eyes, searching for the hot-wax wand.

She stared down at me, beaming. "I just started seeing this badass energy consultant, Angie," Amy said.

"Oh yeah? What's that about?"

"She's helping me readjust where I spend my energy and learn how to manifest more of what I want in life," Amy said. She ripped off a wax strip, and my abs flinched. "I can give you her number, and if you think she can help you, call her."

Since I had no idea what manifesting was all about—or what spirituality was really about, for that matter—I took her number.

It was just past 5:00 p.m. when I left Amy's. I stopped by the movie store on the way home and loaded up on movies that would make me laugh.

Fool's Gold.
Indiana Jones and the Temple of Doom.
The Holiday.
Young Frankenstein.

I drove home and changed into my winter weekend outfit of pajama pants and an oversized sweater. I loaded *Fool's Gold* into my DVD player and plopped down on my couch with my favorite blanket and some chips. After the main characters found their treasure, I preheated the oven and exchanged *Fool's Gold* for *Indiana*. While waiting for the oven to heat up, I made a mental list of what I found attractive about all these male lead roles:

> *Passion for life*
> *Confidence*
> *Strength*
> *Humility*
> *Quick thinking*
> *Ease under stress*

The oven chimed. I loaded my pepperoni pizza into the oven. I started *Indiana Jones and the Temple of Doom* and resumed my position on the couch.

I continued my list of what I adored about these male lead actors.

> *Intelligent*
> *Adventurous*
> *Brave*
> *Sexy*
> *Motivated*
> *Honest*

I imagined what I'd be doing with a man who possessed all the qualities I just rattled off in my head. Definitely not eating pizza, that's for sure. I turned off the television, tossed the remaining pizza into the garbage, and crawled into bed. I rolled over onto my right side and exhaled.

"God, I'm lonely," I said aloud.

Tears piled up under my eyelids, and a cry like none I had ever experienced before came surging up from my rib cage. I couldn't stop crying for several minutes.

"Help me know what to do in life to meet new people," I whispered into the darkness. "To meet new men." I stifled the next sob and drifted asleep.

A mockingbird woke me up the next morning. My silver drapes looked electric in the daylight, and I sat up to check the clock on the far nightstand. The little hand was pointing to the six, and the big hand was somewhere to the right of it. I fell backward and pulled my white, fluffy comforter over my eyes. I let my mind roam, knowing I wasn't going to fall back asleep. My head hurt slightly, which happened on mornings after I'd cried myself to sleep. I searched my emotional spectrum for that lonely feeling. I couldn't find it. I knew it was still within me, though. I lay in bed for a little while longer, listening to the sound of my breath. I inhaled as deeply as I could and held it for several seconds

As I pushed the air out of my body, I imagined healthy, sparkly cells running down into my belly, around my hips, through my legs, knees, calves, ankles, and into my toes. I kicked off the comforter and rolled over to my left side. Slowly, I pushed myself up, stretched my arms high above my head, and reached my fingertips toward the ceiling.

After cracking and popping my wrists, toes, and neck, I finally stood up to twist my spine to the right and then to the left.

The bird was still singing so I pushed the drapes open and tapped on the window to my porch door. "Go away, please."

I headed to the bathroom, splashed water on my face, and smiled at myself in the mirror. The smile was empty, but it felt important to do. Living alone required me to smile at myself in the mirror for my own mental health.

The silence of my home felt heavier since admitting my loneliness the night before.

Once in the kitchen, I went on autopilot. I dropped a cinnamon-spice black tea bag in a colorful ceramic mug my brother and sister-in-law gifted me for Christmas, then placed the last bagel in the toaster. I leaned against the counter, waiting for the water to heat up and the bagel to jump out.

The bagel popped up. I picked it out with the tip of my thumb and index finger, knowing full well it would burn for a few seconds. I slathered on some almond butter and drizzled honey over each side. Taking a moment to inhale all the smells of my breakfast, I tried to connect my breath with my body again. When the water bubbled in the kettle, I filled up my mug and carried everything over to the living room. I settled into the oversized burgundy chair that faced the bay window looking out onto Camelback Mountain.

Mornings matter to me. They are the space between emotions that can easily run me over and rule my mental health. Silence means something different to me in the morning than it does any other part of the day. It wasn't loneliness I felt in the morning. It was hope. I took my time with the bagel and tea, and by the time I could see the bottom of the mug, I was motivated enough to make a plan for the day. It was Sunday Funday, and I could be around people all day long if I wanted to.

But I want to be around the right *people,* I thought to myself. I jumped up and ripped a piece of paper off the Erma Bombeck notepad hanging on the microwave.

Shower.
Church.
Hike.
Mom and Dad's.

I looked over my list. I'd be around people most of the day. Something was still missing. I just didn't know what it was.

I finished *Indiana Jones* and got ready for church. I attended a huge church in Scottsdale. I was one of thousands that attended the mid-morning service. The music was what drew me in and grabbed hold of me. It made my skin tingle and helped me tap into deep emotions I didn't know how to access otherwise. As the offering basket made its way to me, I got out my wallet. Next to a five-dollar bill was the piece of paper Amy had given me. I looked at Angie's number, and my heart crinkled. I felt the same surge of emotion crawling its way back up through my rib cage as I had the night before. I clenched my jaw, pushed my tongue against my teeth, and blinked back the forming tears. The person sitting next to me handed me the offering basket. I cleared my throat, dropped my five-dollar bill into it, and passed it on.

As soon as the song the choir was singing was over, I excused myself from church and turned on my cell phone. I dialed Angie's number as I walked to my car. I got her voice mail.

"Hi, Angie. My name is Carrie Severson," I started. "I got your number from Amy. All she said was if it felt right to call you, I should. So I am. I'm turning thirty soon, and I'm ready to change my life. I'm wondering if you can help me. Please call me at . . ."

I knew she'd play a role in my journey. I didn't know how, but I knew it.

The rest of the day was uplifting. I hiked for an hour, swam in my parents' pool for a bit, and watched *Young Frankenstein* with my sister and my mom as my dad lay in the other room watching World War II clips on television.

I heard my phone chime from the kitchen. I ran to get it and recognized the number as Angie's. There isn't a lot of privacy in my family. Everyone knows everyone else's business, and since I couldn't yet share in complete confidence or detail what I was about to get into with Angie, I took the call into a bedroom on the opposite side of the house.

"Hello, this is Carrie," I said.

"Hi, Carrie. This is Angie."

We agreed that I'd come to her home office for a three-hour session on Monday, February 18, 2008. Later that day, I received an e-mail from Angie that suggested guidelines to maximize my results.

I agreed to cut out alcohol and caffeine for several days prior to working with Angie. I agreed to arrive several minutes ahead of schedule. I agreed to wear something comfortable. I agreed to come with an open heart and a few other things that would help me stay grounded and elevate my energy.

I could barely manage my excitement that day. I had no idea what to expect with Angie, but I wanted the workday to fly by so I could meet her. I worked out during my lunch hour that day, then had lunch at my desk and left ten minutes early so I could get home, change, and arrive at Angie's a handful of minutes early.

I pulled up to Angie's at 5:50 p.m. My heart raced as I walked up to her door. I took two deep breaths and rang the doorbell.

I could see her blond hair and small frame through the opaque glass door as she moved quickly to answer it.

"Carrie!" Angie cheered when she opened the door.

Her bright-blue eyes felt deep. Bottomless. Safe.

I laughed. "Hi, Angie."

Angie grabbed me and pulled me to her for a hug.

"Heart to heart," she said. "Always hug people so that the left cheeks are touching. That way we're both receiving."

I made a mental note and thought of her hug again—heart to heart. *How sweet,* I thought. She guided me to the chair at the head of her dining room table. My back was to a small wooden table that held a large white candle. She handed me a stack of affirmation cards attached to a key ring.

"Read through as many of these cards as you feel guided to, and when you're ready to start, call to me," she said and walked up her spiral staircase.

She turned on some soft instrumental music from upstairs, and I flipped through one card after another.

I am supported.
I see the truth.
I allow myself to receive.
I let go.
I am not a victim.
I am ...
I am ...
I am ...

I read through fifty-four cards and got the idea.

"Angie, I'm ready!"

She slowly climbed down the staircase and joined me at the table, sitting to my right. She asked my permission to video record our conversation. I agreed, and we dug in.

I felt totally vulnerable in front of this stranger. Angie helped me find my footing on this long journey of understanding myself better and becoming a more powerful woman and authentic individual.

Our first time together was intense. I cried deep and hard. After three and a half hours had passed, Angie said it was time to stop. But we had so much more to do. She offered me a thirty-day coaching program, but I didn't feel ready for it.

My time at her table was shocking. I hadn't realized I was burying so much emotion. The idea of diving even deeper into my subconscious and my consciousness was too much at the time.

It took me a few months after my first meeting with Angie to realize I wanted more of her support to transform my life. I went back to her again in May and again in June. Each time we met, I learned something more about myself and what I wanted in life.

I still wanted more, though, and before I left her home in June, I agreed to a six-week coaching program. It was just what I had been looking for. Our contract began on June 6, 2008, and ended on my thirtieth birthday. We focused on certain areas of my life I was committed to improving. We spoke every Monday, and I'd set intentions for the week. We'd reconnect on Friday and talk about what came forward from my intentions and what I was manifesting.

My work with Angie helped me find a new level of confidence and zest for life. I felt more at home with myself. I bought chandeliers for my bedroom and bathroom. I painted cabinets. I began saying thank you to folks who I felt hurt by because I could finally see they did not hold power over me. I adopted a hound dog named Ellie Mae. I met a man. We dated for a year, and I felt sexier and more alive.

This newfound spirituality didn't feel like any other bandwagon I had been on before. It felt like a new way of living. It felt like me.

My first step to get in better alignment with my authentic self was to analyze my relationships. If I was giving to someone and not receiving back, I consciously let those relationships go with surprising ease and grace. I pissed off a few people doing it, too, but the more I let go of the people and the relationships that weighed me down, the lighter I felt and looked. I was more present in my own life and felt clearer throughout the day.

My vocabulary changed, as well as the way I spoke. I would find moments each day to say thank you to anyone who I felt devalued by in some way in order to flip my own energy. I created dream boards for the things I *welcomed* into my life. I learned about the different chakras and practiced energy clearing. I learned about the powerful healing properties of stones, oils, and herbs. And most importantly, I discovered the power of my own intuition.

I also started meditating, which came easily and naturally to me. Learning how to incorporate meditation throughout the day was challenging, though. It wasn't enough for me to be mindful of my body and present in my mind for twenty minutes every morning; I wanted to feel better about my life throughout the day. Meditation even helped me learn how to align my thoughts and feelings with my words and actions. I had to work pretty hard at it.

Writing became an extension of meditation for me. I'd write letters to the Universe every morning. I'd write out intentions and dreams, and ask for the Universe to help me accept whatever came back so I could move closer to those dreams. My work with Angie taught me how to speak to obstacles in life and move mountains with my own thoughts and words.

A year after my work ended with Angie, I surrendered to the fact that I wasn't living my dream life. I was ready to change that, too. I captured my thoughts in a journal one morning in April.

April 7, 2009

Dear Universe,

I want the job of my dreams. Are you waiting for me to say what that is? Is it better if I write "I have the job of my dreams"? Are you waiting for me to tell you what company

I want to work for? I don't know that. I don't really know what I'm supposed to do. I know that I want to focus on well-being and lift others up with my voice. I want to be surrounded by people who promote balance throughout life and teach others how to feel better about themselves. Please help me figure this out.

Love,
Carrie

Chapter Three

THE FOUNDATION

BY THE MIDDLE OF 2009, I KNEW I WAS ON THE BRINK OF A major change in my life. I was as excited for it to start as I was annoyed that it hadn't already started. I've never been a very patient person. I've always felt like I was racing against an invisible ticking time bomb somewhere. My perfectionism and desire to know how things worked out in the end got the best of me fairly often.

One day in July 2009 I had a particularly bad day at the marketing agency I worked at. I wanted to quit my job that very day. Instead, I raced home at 5:00 p.m., changed into my pj's, and grabbed a stack of magazines, a bottle of wine, my favorite glass, a bag of chips, and a journal. I plopped down in the middle of my family room and fanned everything out around me. My dog, Ellie Mae, lay on the pile of magazines and nearly knocked over my wine.

I rubbed Ellie Mae's belly with my left hand, and with the right one I wrote *What am I supposed to do with my life?*

I expected the answers to just come somehow. They didn't.

After half a glass of wine, I grew bored of waiting for answers so I looked through magazines for inspiration.

Luckily for me, I collect magazines. For this little span of my life, it actually worked out perfectly. An advertisement caught my eye and without thinking I tore the page out of the magazine. And something stirred deep in my belly.

Inspiration.

Excitement.

Curiosity.

Wonder.

I went with it and flipped through the magazine faster, ripping out anything that brought on a good feeling. I didn't think about *why* I was intrigued. I just tore out the page and put it in the pile. It was a great exercise in stream-of-consciousness thinking.

After some time, I stopped tearing and reviewed the pile of random pages next to me and Ellie Mae.

In the pile were images of women laughing or exercising or onstage in front of large audiences. Pretty, girlie things I'd like for my home, places I wanted to go visit, and even recipes I wanted to try. Without really thinking about it, I started dividing the pages into different categories based on the emotions I felt when looking at them.

If I felt *happy*, they went into pile A.

If I felt *playful*, they went into pile B.

If I felt *empowered*, they went into pile C.

If I couldn't pinpoint how I felt, I threw them away.

Those were the feelings I wanted to have throughout my career, not just in my personal life. I ended up with several dozen images in piles A, B, and C.

I leaned back against a chair and gazed over them. Ellie Mae and I were relaxed in the stillness and the quiet. Actually, Ellie was snoring pretty bad and I was just staring at the images I had stacked up on my floor. I was convinced these images were somehow going to get me to my next step.

My routine over the next several weeks consisted of rushing home after work, wine, snacks, loud music, and sticking the images up on the walls around my house. I had creative ads for tennis shoes, tampons, and undies. I had images of women cooking together. I had beautiful pictures of couples on horses kissing in a field. I had words, I had articles, I had celebrities. My walls were a melting pot of people, places, and ads.

Does it go without saying that I didn't let anyone into my home during that time?

Well . . . I didn't.

Two months after I started my magazine experiment, I got some answers.

I was in the shower—where, by the way, really amazing ideas come to me—and I heard God say these words: *writing, creative arts, self-esteem,* and *sisterhood*.

All the images I pulled out of magazines flooded my mind. They raced by one image at a time, faster and faster. The images of smiling women popped out almost like a 3D picture. And after a minute or so, those pictures were the only ones I could think about.

I questioned what it was about those images that stuck out right there, and the feelings of being supported and nurtured and happy came over me.

Suddenly, a movie from the nineties called *Indian Summer* came to mind. I've always loved Kevin Pollak and Alan Arkin, but I hadn't thought of the movie since the nineties so I was a little confused why I was randomly thinking of these actors while naked. The fact that it was coming to mind that morning told me I should take notice of it and use it somehow. I just went with it.

"Am I supposed to reach out to Kevin Pollak and Alan Arkin?" I asked God.

I didn't hear a response.

I refocused on the images of women smiling.

New thoughts came to me: *Women supporting women. Women who raise girls who support girls.*

That I could dig into.

Excitement and joy rushed my mind, and goose bumps covered my body.

I could run a girls program and teach them how to be better to one another so they don't bully one another, I thought to myself.

I pictured myself running a summer camp like the movie *Indian Summer.* And then quickly snapped out of it.

"I live in Phoenix," I said to God. "Who would come to Phoenix during the summer?" (Side note: The joke really was on me because, two years later, I launched a nonprofit for girls and our pilot program was held as a summer camp.)

I didn't get a response to that, either. And no other random movie titles, actors, or images came to mind.

Instead, an overwhelming feeling caught hold in my chest. My heart felt as if it were growing right then and there. My whole chest tingled as though it had just woken up after being asleep for some time. It was uncomfortable and a little wearisome. I could feel my heart beating in my ears, behind my eyes, and in my fingernails. I could feel the blood rushing through my body. My head felt very heavy. This really big bubble of emotion grew from my belly into my chest and caught in my throat. The tears welled up behind my eyes, and I laughed and sobbed at the same time. I was a total mess, and for once, I was grateful to be alone.

It was simultaneously amazing and terrifying. I didn't hear God say anything to me, but I knew in my heart, gut, mind, and soul that if I wanted to change the way girls treated girls, I was going to have to create a fun program for them. I was going to have to become an entrepreneur.

And it actually made sense to me. I had never really been any good at staying at a job longer than two years anyway.

How I was going to change society for girls and women was a question I didn't know the answer to.

How I was going to help girls and women create a stronger sense of sisterhood in their lives was something else I didn't know the answer to.

How I was going to help girls and women enhance their self-esteem was also a question that came to mind. I didn't know the answer to that, either.

But I knew that whatever I was going to create would be for the greater good of females, and *that* was what I was supposed to do with my life.

The next eighteen months of my life were dedicated to looking for answers to the big *HOW* questions. As I had throughout my twenties when I was searching for myself, I jumped in with full faith and I ran full speed ahead. This time around, I was looking for some company.

I decided to call my friend Eileen. She and I had met at Arizona State University, and we were pretty united in how we felt about all things that had to do with girls being shitty to one another.

"I think I know what I'm supposed to do with my life," I said to Eileen.

"Oh good. What?" she asked.

"I'm supposed to create a company that helps girls be more supportive of one another," I said.

"That makes sense," Eileen said.

"Will you help me?"

"Sure!"

Eileen had three children and absolutely no time to help me figure out my life, but she was—and still is—someone I could always turn to when I needed a partner. She's a soul sister, for sure, someone I can go six months without talking to and then pick our friendship right back up. She's part of my personal foundation. The best part about our friendship is that I know I don't have to ask if she feels the same way about me.

She's the type of friend I wanted girls to grow up to be and the kind of friend I wanted them to have.

For months and months on end, I'd call Eileen on Friday and ask if I could work from her kitchen table. She always agreed.

Between researching and playing with her kids, we'd talk about new recipes we wanted to make or new workouts we wanted to try. It was a unique way to move into an incubator phase for this company I wanted to create, and it worked. I researched companies around the world that were offering healthy lifestyle programs for girls. Whenever I came across something profound, I'd read it off to Eileen as she was making meals or folding laundry.

I printed articles at home or at work over the next several months. I had folders filled with pieces about girls' self-esteem, bullying, and creative art programs.

Having one person know what I was doing at night and on the weekends was comforting. I didn't feel alone in it. And it gave me accountability. I couldn't back out of it now, and when I struggled, I had someone there to help me stay the course.

I hit a wall a few months into the journey. I was back on my living room floor with Ellie Mae and some wine. I was in my pajamas rubbing Ellie's belly again and reviewing all my research. I read stories about girls in Africa, stories about education budget cuts in Arizona, stories about girls cutting themselves, and stories about after-school centers closing down. I read hundreds upon hundreds of stories. I was past the point of research. I knew there was a place in the world for what I wanted to create. I just didn't know where to go next.

The Universe works in very weird ways for me. I get messages in the most random places. While in meditation one day, I saw Angie's blue eyes. Our work together was always deep and intense, and I trusted her. So I found myself back at her kitchen table on July 30, 2009.

"I know what I want to do with my life," I said to her when we started.

And it just poured out of me.

"It'll be a nonprofit for girls. We'll write, and we'll do creative classes. We can offer dance classes and cooking classes. And the girls will learn how to talk to one another in a supportive way. It'll be an after-school program, and we'll work with girls around the country."

Angie was thrilled for me, and our session felt more like two badass entrepreneurs talking than it did a coaching session. She suggested I interview nonprofit leaders over the next several months and find out what was working for their organizations and what wasn't.

So I did. I spoke with a nonprofit leader once a week for five months.

In 2009, nonprofits were hit hard financially. The leaders I spoke to were being expected to do more because of layoffs, but people were giving less because of the economy. After-school programs were shutting down. Day care centers were folding. Creative arts classes at schools were being cut. And I was in the wings wanting to create a program for girls that most likely would be held after school and incorporate the creative arts somehow.

At the start of 2010, I decided to look at this new idea of mine as I would a new marketing client's. I had done the research already, and I had spoken to dozens of people in town who all said the same things: Businesses were hard work, and nonprofits were harder. I was insane to launch one. I'd fail. Nonprofits didn't make any money. Creative arts nonprofits made even less money. The economy was shit. I should go back to school and become a social worker.

But I knew in my heart there was a market for a girls program that supported self-esteem and creative arts. I just couldn't prove it. What were girls looking for? What were parents looking for? What would I tell a client to do to learn about their market? I knew the answer to that. I'd tell a client to pay a company to do actual market research.

So I did.

I reached out to a woman I'd met in yoga years earlier. I knew she worked for a market research firm in town that was hired to survey people and report on the findings. We met at a Starbucks on a Saturday. I brought my binder with all the research I had printed over the years and the notes from all my interviews, as well as a short business plan with a mission and vision statement.

With her help, we drafted up a twenty-five-question survey that would go out to five hundred parents in the Phoenix area who had daughters ages six through thirteen.

Did the parents send their child(ren) to an after-school program?

If not, would they?

Did the family engage in physical activity outdoors?

Would the parents be interested in enrolling their daughters in a program that enhanced their self-esteem?

We sent out the survey on a Monday in January 2010, and the results came back the next month. I had the proof I needed. Whatever I was building for girls had a place in Phoenix. Parents were looking for what I was creating.

Throughout 2010, I listened to music from the eighties to put me back in the mindset of my childhood to ensure that what I created would have a childlike quality to it.

For the next three months, I met with entrepreneurs who could shine light on how to start a business. And for four months after that, I held focus groups at my home for twenty people at a time. I pitched them things like logos, program concepts, and pricing, and I asked them for their honest feedback.

The August 2010 focus group brought on the biggest shift for me on this start-up journey. Eileen and my sister, Holly, came over earlier that Saturday afternoon to help me get ready for it. I served turkey meatballs and quinoa, and a raw strawberry cobbler for dessert. This particular focus group covered everything from who we should serve to the name of the nonprofit. I specifically wanted to know if people thought we should only focus on girls in low economic areas or on all girls.

Guests arrived on time and brought their own beverages, as requested. Really close friends of mine brought me little gifts, which made the night a little easier on me. Guests helped themselves to dinner and sat in my living room. Once everyone was seated and comfortable, Ellie Mae and I sat down in the middle of my living room floor and looked up at them all.

"Thanks for coming, everyone," I said. "Think of this as a working think tank."

I knew in my heart I was creating an organization for girls, yet I was looking for confirmation from my peers that an organization only focusing on girls was okay to do.

So I asked the people sitting in my home that night their thoughts on only supporting girls.

The women all loved the idea. The nonprofit leaders in the room had a more structured way to look at it and gave me answers having to do with my mission and how I would raise money. And finally, all eyes zeroed in on the only man in the room.

"It's a smart approach," he said.

All my peers confirmed this big leap for me, and I got what I was looking for.

Next up was the name of the organization. Eileen, Holly, and I had taped up three different possible names of the organization around my home.

The Soul School.

Nitty-Gritty.

Back to Basics.

All twenty individuals at my home that night voted a strong *no* to all three options. Then my friend Megan, who was finishing up her strawberry cobbler, said, "Carrie, you should just put your name on it and call it a day."

She put her bowl down on the table and looked at me. She was serious. The room was silent. I looked at my feet and thought about it. The idea of naming the nonprofit after myself had never crossed my mind. In fact, it felt uncomfortable at first.

I thanked everyone for coming and handed out my home-made strawberry cobbler recipe as a thank-you gift. Eileen and

Holly helped me clean up and take the trash out before they left. I crawled into bed and drifted asleep shortly after.

I woke up the next morning to the sight of Ellie Mae doing a downward dog stretch next to my bed, which meant I had another few seconds before I had to get up to take her outside. I took a deep breath and stretched out my body on the mattress. My breath contracted in my chest when the phrase *Severson Sisters* crossed my mind.

It rolled through my thoughts loud and clear, and tears welled in my eyes as I exhaled. Chills ran up and down my entire body. I knew, without question, that Severson Sisters was meant to be the name of my nonprofit. I knew it. Whether or not I had the guts to *actually* name it after myself was the hurdle on the horizon.

I rolled out of bed, splashed water on my face, and took Ellie Mae out for a brief morning stroll as the sun was just tipping over the horizon.

Ellie Mae was my best friend, and I told her about everything.

"Pumpkin Face, what do you think about the name Severson Sisters for the nonprofit?" I asked. I said it over and over again.

Severson Sisters.

Severson Sisters.

Severson Sisters.

The more I said it, the more emotionally connected to it I felt. After the sixth or seventh time saying it out loud, I cried, and then a wall of anxiety hit me. Ellie and I finished our morning walk just in time for the blazing heat of August in Phoenix to spread across the city.

Before Ellie and I went inside our home, I stood on the back porch and took a deep breath. I reached my arms up to the sky and prayed for a sign. "Please, God, help me let go of all fear and anxiety about creating Severson Sisters and naming it after me and Holly."

Ellie was jumping at the door, ready to go in. She got her breakfast and all the goodies that came with it, and I filled the teakettle. I stood against the counter and waited for the water to warm up. Ellie looked over her shoulder every few bites to make sure I was still there watching her.

I poured myself a cup of tea and sent Eileen a text containing only two words: *Severson Sisters.*

She responded immediately. *That's it!*

I climbed into the big burgundy chair in the living room and slowly sipped my tea. I wrote a letter to the Universe and called my sister. We made a plan to swim that morning before the heat made it impossible to enjoy being outdoors.

Instead of attending church that morning, I danced. I danced to the eighties music station on television. I bounced and twirled around. I screamed as loud as I could to the tune playing. I laughed, and I cried, and I let myself experience the morning as fully as I could.

I saw Holly pull up the driveway, and as I watched her walk to the back door, I prepared myself. As she opened the door the song "We Built This City" came on the station. I was standing in the center of my living room when she came in, and she knew something was on my mind.

"What's wrong?" Holly asked.

"I know the name of the company."

"What is it?"

"Severson Sisters."

Holly screamed and laughed and cried all at the same time.

"Are you okay with that?" I asked.

"Are you sure?"

"Yes."

"Then yes!"

We hugged it out in my dining room and walked out to the pool. I didn't know anything else other than the name of the non-profit, that we'd offer a girls program, and that we'd help girls all over the country. Everything else was a mystery.

I was just months away from my life never being the same, and I didn't even know it, let alone plan for it.

Chapter Four

LEAP OF FAITH

FACED MY FEAR OF BEING AN ENTREPRENEUR THROUGH MY spiritual practice throughout the rest of 2010. I filed paperwork for Severson Sisters in December 2010, and I always came back to my meditation practice and my writing.

Sometimes the words in my journals were tokens of appreciation. Other times, the words were a cry for help. Some journal entries were letters to God. I wrote to my future husband in some entries. I wrote to myself. I wrote to people I needed to forgive. I wrote to my body. I wrote to my heart. I wrote to angels and fairies and anything or anyone else that came to mind.

I waited for answers. Once I heard them, I took action. By December 2010 I was very certain I was ready to launch.

December 1, 2010

Dear Universe,

My intentions for this month are as follows:

- *I release all worry I have about the future.*
- *I connect to my body through my higher self in a balanced way as I move from parties and celebrations.*
- *I ask to be let go from the agency I currently work for and begin my career as a nonprofit leader.*

Leaps of faith happen for me all the time. I look at every decision I make as a leap of faith. After writing that third intention down, I got an idea. If I wanted something, I had to act as if it were already in my life. I prayed to be released from the job I had because I felt trapped.

For more than a month, I removed something personal from my desk—CDs, photos, journals, my plant, artwork—before I left work every night. That way, when the day finally came to be released, I would be able to grab my purse and walk out the front door. I was preparing my life for a manifestation. Nobody noticed. I don't think anyone really cared.

The marketing agency I worked for lost a major account before Christmas. As the lowest-billable employee, I knew it was only a matter of time before I was let go.

I was laid off around 3:00 p.m. on January 12. It wasn't a surprise. I happened to stand up to stretch my legs and noticed the office manager meandering nearby, staring at me. She never did that. My boss peered around the corner of my cubicle and asked me to come into a corner conference room. My heart leaped. *It was finally happening!* After my boss let me go and went over the details, I went back to my office, grabbed my purse and walked out for the last time.

My first thought after driving out of the parking garage was, *it's happy hour.* And I couldn't think of a better reason to have a cocktail in the middle of the afternoon. I drove to the closest bar and sat down. I was the only person there.

"What'll you have?" the bartender asked me.

"It feels like a cosmo kind of day for me."

It was familiar. It was safe. It was easy. Carrie Bradshaw would have had the same thing on a day like that.

He placed the bright-pink drink down in front of me and went about his duties. I leaned over the bar, placed my lips on the glass, and took a long sip of the cranberry concoction. Then I called my dad.

I told him about my day. He offered to pay for a headhunting service. I declined. He insisted. I declined again. He would book the appointment for me. My dad's response was how I imagine most dads would respond. He panicked about the money. More specifically, he wanted to know where I'd make it and why what I was creating had to be a nonprofit.

I called my mom next.

I think my mom's response was similar to how most moms would respond if their daughter lost a job. She was flat-out pissed at my old boss. I let my dad take on the fear of the unknown for me while my mom took on the fear of letting go.

I drove home and collected my mail. Among the typical letters and promo flyers, there was an envelope from the Arizona

Corporation Commission. Inside was the official letter stating that Severson Sisters had been accepted as a 501(c)(3) nonprofit organization by the state of Arizona.

There was no turning back after that.

I put every cent of my 401(k) and savings into the creation, launch, and start-up costs for Severson Sisters—a total of $35,000.

Despite the fact that I had spent eighteen months in what I fondly call my "research and development stage," I really didn't know what I was doing. I had volunteered for nonprofits before, but I'd never run one. I sat on boards to govern nonprofits, but being the CEO was different—especially when the nonprofit was only made up of one person.

My dad gifted me a space in his office to call the Severson Sisters headquarters. Each morning for the next ninety days consisted of writing website copy, interviewing candidates for both an advisory board and governing board, and putting together a pilot program.

I hid behind the scenes of this brand-new company I created—an empowerment organization for girls focused on inspiring them to live as their awesome, authentic, super selves. The program was called Super Girl, and it would offer anti-bullying solutions to middle-school girls, as well as empowerment tips and tools. And we were going to start it all as a summer program in Phoenix, Arizona.

Little did I know that by taking this leap of faith, my life would change. Fast. Drastically. And sometimes dramatically.

My letters to the Universe guided me the entire way.

March 25, 2011

Dear Universe,

I am joyful today. I feel supported everywhere I go. I am at peace. I am joyful when I meditate, dance, pamper myself by doing my nails, going for walks, sleeping in, and cuddling with my dog. I feel empowered, as well, as I'm creating an organization for young girls with the money I've been saving for years. I'm a little scared, though. Please send me board members I can trust in this new journey.

What can I do to ease my fear?

Connect and talk to people I love.

Connect to me more.

Rest more.

Answer these questions: What does a girl in your program look like? What does she get out of it? What will she do? What are your motivators for launching Severson Sisters and this Super Girl program?

Tell your story.

Later that month, I was sitting in my office and logged on to a social media site to waste time, and I caught a press conference happening at the White House. The First Lady declared her platform as bullying prevention, and she announced her big initiative.

I sat there, paralyzed. Soon, paralysis turned to excitement. I clicked through our website in awe of how aligned Severson Sisters Super Girl was with what I had just heard from the White House.

The following Monday I knew it was time. I wasn't totally ready to share what I had been working on for months, but I still followed the intuitive nudges I was getting. I hit the "publish" button on our website and pulled up a social media site. Before I could talk myself out of it, I posted a super quick, easy-breezy statement about starting this new nonprofit, how I was excited for this next adventure, and shared the new website. I grabbed my water bottle, keys, and sunglasses off the table, and left my house. I didn't want to wait for a response to my post. Without thinking about where I was going or what I was doing, I drove to the gym. Luckily for me, an aerobics class was just starting. I popped inside the exercise room and hung out in the back so nobody would notice me hyperventilating in the corner. I had purposely left my phone at home so I could create space for myself to work out all the worries and concerns I had about taking this leap of faith known. It didn't really work, but at least I bounced around and sweat a little bit.

I was the first one out of the room and got home in record time. I threw open the patio door, pressed a button on my computer to wake it up, and hit "refresh" on the social media site. Dozens and dozens of comments waited for me. People were really surprised. Most were supportive. My family was worried about how I'd pay bills and buy groceries. It felt like it had really started. I couldn't turn back.

Come the middle of April, just weeks after I made Severson Sisters known to the public, I booked a television segment. It was my first time on a morning television show, and I was so excited. It was the fastest four minutes of my life. I didn't wear enough makeup, and I interrupted the reporter—all things on the what-not-to-do-on-live-television list.

The cameraman notified us that we were on commercial break. I stood up and clapped, and hugged the woman who had interviewed me. I stood there listening to her feedback. She was midsentence when a producer introduced himself to me and the production assistant unclipped the microphone from my shirt and grabbed the battery pack from my jeans pocket. The producer booked me on two more shows for the following week and ushered me off the set. It all happened so fast.

My phone rang when I got to my car. It was a leader of a local girls group who wanted Super Girl at her next meeting. I turned her down because we wanted to run our pilot program before offering our services to any outside groups.

I received three other phone calls like that within the month. We also had thirty-five parents enroll their daughters in a summer camp session before June 5, 2011.

Over the course of the next two months, my levels of anxiety and excitement were pretty equal. The money I had used to launch Severson Sisters was gone by the time the pilot program started, and for the rest of 2011, I lived on credit cards and whatever money Severson Sisters brought in. I took a 55 percent pay cut to launch Severson Sisters, and I had no idea when—or if— money would flow back into my life.

I was running on pure faith that this direction was the right one.

June 5, 2011

Dear Universe,

It's the day before Severson Sisters Super Girl starts its pilot program. I know you're here with me. I know you're leading me. What I'm disconnected with is money. When are you bringing financial flow to Severson Sisters? What more can I do to gain it? What can I do to step into my power in a way that attracts abundance?

Our six-week pilot program wrapped in August 2011, right before the kids returned to school. Since bullying was in the national spotlight, I was called on by the local media—often—for more information and my thoughts on a few recurring questions:

How can you help your child deal with bullies when returning to school?

Where can girls get into Severson Sisters Super Girl this school year?

What's the difference between boys' and girls' bullying behavior?

The more media exposure we gained, the bigger the demand was for the Severson Sisters Super Girl program—and the more critical the public became of what we offered.

- *Why aren't you doing this for boys?*
- *When are you coming to upstate New York?*
- *Why aren't you offering anything for girls in math and sciences?*
- *Why is it only a one-time workshop?*
- *What does my daughter do now?*
- *Can you come to our school every Tuesday?*
- *What are you doing about bullying in the workplace?*
- *Can you offer a Severson Sisters Super Girl program at my home?*
- *Are you offering a program for incarcerated women?*

- *Can you create a workshop for the girls in my group?*
- *Can you offer your program for free?*
- *Can you offer your Severson Sisters Super Girl program to our girls once a week this fall?*

For every positive comment I received, I also received a negative one. As the conductor of the Severson Sisters Super Girl train, I took the heat in a way board members and volunteers didn't. We were supported tremendously, and the community drank us up. It felt as if I were being consumed, too. And that's when the suffocation started. I had no boundaries. I wore this organization like it was my own skin. And just a year into it, I could already feel that skin drying and cracking.

When January 2012 hit, I experienced my first bout of panic. Ellie Mae had passed away just days before Christmas, and I was alone for the first time in years. I now understand that the timing of her passing was a blessing. Severson Sisters erupted in 2012, and it totally stole most of my time, with so little left over for myself. There was zero space available for anyone or anything else.

By the end of January 2012, I had put on twenty-five additional pounds. Most of my journal entries in the beginning of 2012 were written to and from my body. The pace I ran at was really taking a toll on me. I was fatigued all the time, and I couldn't afford the foods I knew would fuel me to the greatest good so, oftentimes I ate cheap sandwiches.

January 23, 2012

Body,

Why am I ashamed of our figure?

Because you feel unworthy of love at this size.

I don't mean to feel unworthy of love, though. It's actually what I welcome in the most. And feeling unworthy of love at any size isn't something I'm intentionally doing to us. And I don't want to. I don't want to hold on to that thought pattern.

I know all this.

This weight that came on is heavy for us to carry. When we let go of feeling unworthy of love, it'll all come off.

How can I do that, though?

Cry. Be kind to yourself. Honor yourself in all your actions. Stop drinking. Stop hanging on to what other people think of what you created. Cook again. Come out and play more. Let your light show up again. You can do this.

I sometimes don't even have the money to buy healthy food, though. You're telling me how to live as if I had money to support myself. Give me money, and I'll be able to take better care of us.

Knowing the power that words have over us, sometimes I wrote as if I already had the perfect body, business, relationships, and life.

February 2, 2012

Carrie,

We are perfect. We are loved and supported by the Universe. We will succeed this morning because we've done it in the past. We win over these potential donors. We are on such a powerful ride of feminine energy and receive abundantly. With the abundance we receive today, we are able to pay our bills easily and gracefully, buy healthy foods, and take care of ourselves. It is safe to release this weight, as it no longer serves us. I love us from a deep place, and I accept who we are, where we are, and what we look like.

Lovingly,

Me

But by the end of February 2012, I was unable to pay my first bill. I was furious at God. I asked for help. I asked for money. I asked for companionship. What I wanted more than anything was someone to come home to and share my life with. I wanted a man to hold me and tell me it was going to be okay. I hadn't even been on a date since the organization started.

Thankfully, my girlfriends are badasses. Most of them are spiritual and business savvy, and could handle what I had to unload. In the first few years of running Severson Sisters, my emotional scale included depression, extreme anxiety, absolute bliss, and what I labeled grief.

One girlfriend, Dawn, gifted me with bimonthly coaching calls to help me with my mental health.

"What can you do for yourself to reduce the financial burden? Is there anything you can get rid of?" Dawn asked one day.

I was still paying for a gym membership. And health insurance. And cable. After that conversation, I got rid of it all and was left $400 a month lighter. That helped a little. But a month later, the financial suffocation moved beyond me and grabbed hold of Severson Sisters. I felt such guilt for being a financial burden on the company. And at the same time, I was so pissed that the organization couldn't pay me regularly. As the nonprofit gained more exposure, my life became even more chaotic. I blamed myself for being a "media darling" without the ability to secure ongoing financial support.

My life was a roller coaster. The highs were awesome, but the dips were dangerous and severe and always lasted longer than the highs.

One of the highest highs came on March 7, 2012, when I received an e-mail from an editor at a women's fashion magazine.

Hi, Carrie,

CONGRATULATIONS! You have been chosen as a winner of our 2012 "Best of You" Contest. Each year, we recognize four outstanding women who give their all to help their communities and make the world a better place. We are so excited that you have been chosen to be a part of this extraordinary experience.

It was exactly what I needed to hear. I received a round-trip ticket to New York City and was given the opportunity to bring a guest. We would stay in a boutique hotel for two nights. We'd receive spending cash, a haircut or color, and a manicure and pedicure, and we were asked to participate in an ad campaign that would appear in the magazine.

My mom came to New York City to celebrate with me. On the day of the actual photo shoot, I gathered with the three other ladies featured by the contest and our guests, and we watched as a crew turned an empty loft in lower Manhattan into a photography studio.

The hair and makeup crew took over one section of the space. The photographer and her lighting equipment set up near the windows in the back. And the other wall became a pop-up dressing room filled with four different racks of dresses.

I changed out of my street clothes, put on an oversized robe, and climbed into a chair in the hair-and-makeup section of the loft. One woman straightened my hair. Another woman put on my makeup. A third woman painted my nails. Before I was finished, the photographer's assistant asked me what type of music I'd like playing during my photo shoot.

"I like classic rock," I said.

"Can you give me a band?"

"How about the Rolling Stones?"

"Perfect."

I was the last one to get photographed. A stylist helped me into a light-pink gown and shoes a size too small for my feet. As she buckled my feet into the heels, my playlist started. "Start Me Up" by the Rolling Stones blared through the loft. I heard the photographer yell over the music and asked the assistant to turn it up even louder. The energy in the room felt fuller. I felt like a queen, a warrior, a badass, and a goddess as I walked over to have my picture captured.

An *X* was taped on the ground, and I took my position. I smiled, turned, laughed, and had the most fun. A man kneeled down next to the lights and aimed a gigantic fan at me for that windblown effect. My mom was even able to join me for a few photos, and we cherished that moment together.

After the last photograph was taken, I was asked to join the set producer in an adjoining room. She was working on a behind-the-scenes video for the magazine. "What does this experience mean to you?" she asked me.

I took a few beats to think about that. I repeated the question and let my eyes focus out the window at the Hudson River. A small statue caught my eye, and I quickly realized I was looking at Lady Liberty. My eyes glazed over with tears instantly. I turned to the producer. "This experience feels like an opportunity, and I'm so grateful. I really am," I said, just before the tears started to fall. It felt like they were years old, and they just kept coming. I excused myself and stepped out of the shot.

The magazine experience was beautiful. My dad paid for my mom and me to stay a few extra days in Manhattan so we could see *Wicked* and enjoy ourselves. My brother even took the train in from Pittsburgh to join in our celebration.

I fed off the energy of that experience for months until the next big high came in.

During one of my mental health check-ins with Dawn, she asked me to describe the experience in a few words.

I chose *nice, gentle,* and *fun.*

Then she recommended I do nice, gentle, fun things for myself each day.

I made a mental note of nice things:

Flowers
Reading fiction books

I made a list of gentle things:

Stretching
Taking an hour by myself for lunch without working
Baths
No work on the weekends

I made a list of fun things:

Dancing in the living room
Conversations with my friends
Painting

Taking an hour to sit down in the middle of the day to have lunch by myself was an easy adjustment. Turning on music to dance it out in my living room was a no-brainer. Disconnecting from work on the weekends was a challenge.

The more space I gave myself to breathe, the easier it was to see that the money I did have could go toward supporting my overall health.

My first step was to see a naturopathic team. I was paired with a doctor who specialized in homeopathic care. She treated me for deep emotional strains that were clouding and polluting my mind and body. We worked together to treat, release, clear, and heal all aspects of my body—physical, emotional, and mental.

After an initial panel of blood work, the naturopath told me that my thyroid had quit doing its job, my cortisol level was three times too high, and my adrenal glands had stopped supporting me.

She recommended I start taking a homeopathic remedy to address extreme anxiety, in addition to a few supplements.

One day in her office, she asked me a series of questions to nail down the right remedy for me to start. All her questions had to do with Severson Sisters and stress. And then she got to this one: *Do you resent taking that initial leap of faith?*

I felt a lump develop in my throat. I kept staring at her, waiting for the emotion caught in my throat to pass. She leaned back in her chair and watched me. She gave me a tender smile and nodded. Out came this deep, ugly cry. It was a cry I didn't know was there or was ready to come up.

But there it was.

Resentment.

It was a deep-rooted emotion for me. I was so caught off guard by the workload and the financial strain of Severson Sisters, and I constantly felt and thought that help was on the way, only to be repeatedly disappointed. It was that cycle that led to feeling resentful.

Part of my treatment plan with the naturopath was to meditate twice a day and mindfully work on taking deeper breaths whenever I felt stressed.

To help bring in big highs more often, I leaned in more to my spiritual practice and meditated twice a day.

My morning practice was always the same. I saw myself on a beach. I was at peace and could feel peace in my body.

My afternoon or evening practice was usually a bit different. I saw myself standing at the ocean's edge, on a cliff, facing a heavy storm. And I could feel it. I knew I was standing in what felt like the beginning of the storm. But I'd signed up for this. I'd created this organization. One of my missions in life was to bring Severson Sisters to the world, and I couldn't understand why I was struggling so hard and why it was feeling like I was in it all alone.

My credit cards were maxed out, too, which meant I had to create new ways to make money. I was so worried about what other people would say if I got a job to relieve the financial burden. I was worried that if I leaned back a little, people would consider me a failure.

Running was my first response, and since I was the one holding myself captive, I ran so fast that nobody could relate to me. I ran so fast that I felt isolated. I ran so fast that nobody could hear me. And I blamed everyone else for being unable to relate to me, unable to hear me, unable to help me.

Despite the fact that I heard messages of hope in meditation and recorded them in my writing, I still felt a burning need to do more. No matter what came in, though, it wasn't enough. I thought someone would eventually come along and help.

October 1, 2012

Dear Universe,

What should I do today about my personal finances?

Ask the newspaper for writing assignments, if you want to. Money is coming in to support you this month. No need to stress. All is well. Enjoy. Relax and celebrate.

I need to pay my bills, though. Help me do that.

Create new pathways for yourself. What's outside this box of yours? Create. Bring yourself to the people. Consult, if you want. Empower others. Empower women. You are Carrie Severson. You are the creator of Severson Sisters. You are smart. You are business oriented. You can give what you've created to women. All you have to do is create it. Create self-esteem and business-esteem workshops. Connect to people and businesses that are spiritually based. Work on your relationships. Make the decision and move into the creative energy. Money and connections will come in for you, though, so ease up on how hard you're being on yourself.

Can you give me specifics?

Release your attachment to what your path is supposed to look like. The truth is, you'll keep going after your dreams so just keep moving forward.

Appreciate the support you have.

Cut cords to pity.

Release energy to pain and your past.

Be present.

Ask a man out on a date if you want to go on a date.

Accept whatever transpires, and be thankful.

By that point in my entrepreneurial journey, I was in a constant state of overdrive and well on my way to burnout. The harder I fought for Severson Sisters, the more intense the roller coaster became. I knew I was disconnected even as I was in the heart of the storm and sprinting toward burnout.

But what I was feeling and what I was presenting to the public were two different things. The public knew me as this light. Most referred to me as "the Super Girl Lady." Very few close personal friends knew that I was drowning.

November 4, 2012

Dear Universe,

I can feel the storm lessening. I can feel a release coming in. I am ready for the harvest. I know I am blessed by grace. I know this organization is meant to be here for girls. Today, I ask you to walk in front of me on my path and speak louder and show yourself in bigger ways. I ask to be freed of this worry and money block. Please give me the strength and motivation to align myself with my own truth, with your truth for me. I ask you to help me shed this protective barrier I've created for myself. Its weight. Its heaviness. It's deep-rooted, and I no longer want it. I want the strength to release it easily. I release all shields that hold me in a fear pattern. I ask to be free of everything that clutters my truth.

When 2013 rolled in, however, I was nowhere close to where I thought I'd be. It was my thirty-fifth year on this planet, and all I could feel was disappointment.

March 23, 2013

God,

I love you, but I'm pissed at you right now. You're putting me under so much financial strain right now. I've asked you repeatedly for months now to send support. We need financial support to pay for a staff so I can put some of this workload onto other people and start to take care of myself. The weight I'm putting on is related to stress, and without financial support, the stress increases and the weight increases, too. Send checks today.

I ask for $250,000 a year for Severson Sisters to have a full staff of three people. Thank you for sending in financial support.

Thank you for the abundance of volunteers who are coming to help us put on a Super Girl program with a hundred girls next week.

And as always, Spirit, thank you for sending in my life partner today. I could use his help.

Help me stay open so I can hear you better today.

My requests hadn't been answered for months. I was angry at God for leading me down this deserted, barren path that brought me to this place of pain and exhaustion.

When I launched Severson Sisters, I had felt called by God to do so. He had closed the door to the marketing agency and showed me the window from which to take that leap of faith. I had been nervous but so aligned with His mission for me. Two years later, His mission felt like a burden I was meant to carry, and the weight of the organization was numbing me.

And as it turns out, numbness is an emotion! Well, it was for me. It was the first sign that I had burned out. I couldn't feel anymore. I was on an autopilot with a broken emergency brake.

I looked at the media segments as an obligation because they never brought in any money. I looked at the free workshops we were asked to put on or be a part of as our responsibility because our mission was to serve girls and we should do that any way we could. And I was at the helm of it all. I managed the interns. I managed the events. I did all 150 media segments. I managed the board. I did everything, and I did it the very best I could. But at some point, I stopped believing my best was good enough.

I made it through 2012 by taking home $16,000 from Severson Sisters, cashing in on life insurance policies my grandparents had taken out on me, accepting money from my parents, and maxing out my credit cards. It took me five years to pay off the debt I had accumulated from this leap of faith I had been so determined to make.

Chapter Five

HEADING HOME

I WENT SKYDIVING IN MY EARLY TWENTIES. I REMEMBER THE feeling well. I scooted my way up to the open door and leaned forward just a few inches and was essentially sucked out of the plane. I was free-falling toward the ground.

The sensation of gravity pushing down against the air made it hard to breathe. My body felt limitless, yet my lungs burned.

The man I was skydiving tandem with yelled into my ear, "Scream so I know you didn't check out."

Nothing came.

"Use your diaphragm and push air out."

I engaged my belly and got out one short scream. There was this constant pressure pushing against me, and there was nothing I could do. I was definitely running on adrenaline.

That rush of adrenaline is what I felt most days while running Severson Sisters. From the moment I launched it I moved as fast as I could without knowing what I was really doing. There were days I couldn't inhale deeply enough to feel the relief of a full exhale. There were days I felt like I was crawling through a barren desert filled with empty wells. And what crushed my spirit the most was the fact that I was doing everything everyone asked of me and I never felt satisfied.

I'd go around the Phoenix area to talk to groups, and I was constantly asked why I didn't launch a program for boys. My answer was always the same: *I don't know what it's like to grow up as a boy. I can tell you what it's like to be a girl, though, and I can help girls growing up today.*

What I wanted to say was: *I did an amazing thing. You go launch a program for boys. What I created was totally enough.*

We'd also hold programs at community centers, most of which were free. It was difficult to offer these things for free with the state of Severson Sisters' finances, but the few times we did put a price tag on them, people just complained. I didn't know how to avoid the pitfalls of burnout and, as a result, suffocation. I said yes to everything and put myself dead last. I couldn't stop long enough to catch my breath, take care of me, and flip my world around. Everything I did was for Severson Sisters. And everything in my personal life suffered because of it.

It all came to a head in June 2013.

Two important people in my life were at major milestones in their lives.

My dear friend Jennifer was marrying her best friend in the backyard of a Beverly Hills home in early June, and another dear friend, Celeste, was celebrating her fortieth birthday at the end of June with a girls' trip to Nashville. Both these occasions were important to them, and both were just as important to me.

But I didn't have enough money to attend, and all my cards were still maxed out. I tried to get several different new credit cards, but because my credit had been ruined, I couldn't get one.

So I did the only thing I could think of: Severson Sisters took out a new credit card, and I put the two plane tickets on that, deciding I would pay it off personally.

A friend who was going to the wedding called and asked if I was staying with anyone at the hotel. Obviously, I had no idea where I was going to stay because I couldn't *afford* to stay there. Thankfully, she offered to spot my stay, and we agreed I would pay her back later.

I was very grateful to her, but the fact that I couldn't afford to celebrate with a friend on her wedding day or with another as she moved through a major life milestone was my breaking point.

I needed to stop running. I knew healing was the only option I had left.

I woke up on June 1, 2013, and took control of my life in a way I'd never done before. The grip I'd had around my resentment, anger, shame, guilt, and suffocation loosened. I felt desperate for a change, and somehow I knew it was just around the corner.

Later that day I went to my office to wrap up a few things before heading out of town for most of June. My dad walked in as I was getting things sorted and stood leaning against the wall across from me. His blue eyes widened slightly when an honest conversation was on his mind, and that's what they did in that moment. He asked me about my upcoming travels and if I needed any money for my trips.

My heart tightened in my chest, and every emotion I had been hiding formed a large lump at the bottom of my throat. My parents had already booked me a plane ticket back to Wisconsin for the summer, and I was already carrying guilt around from that. The truth was, I did need the money because what was in my personal bank account or the organization's wasn't enough to even leave the airport.

I swallowed. "I could use some cab money to get to and from the airport."

"Is that it? That can't be it, Carrie," my dad said.

The lump dissolved, and tears gushed out in an instant. I collapsed onto my desk and sobbed. "I'm so sorry, Dad. I'm trying my best. I don't understand why it's this hard," I said.

He rubbed my back and hugged me to him. "I know you are, Carrie. It'll come together. Let me do this. I know you need some money, and you need to take a break and be with your friends."

I stopped crying. I just shut it off. There was a ton more there. I knew it. I bet my dad knew it. But I wasn't ready to face it or let it out just then. I wiped the tears from my face and nodded. My dad peeled off some bills and handed them to me. I tucked them away in my wallet and swallowed whatever pride I still had. My dad smiled at me, gave me a thumbs-up, and walked out of my office.

I couldn't concentrate on anything after that. In my wallet, I had what I needed to celebrate my friends, but only because my father had given it to me. I e-mailed the board of directors to let them all know I needed a break. They each had assignments to check on, e-mails to answer in my stead, schedule programs that needed to happen, and pay whatever bills came in while I was taking my break. I set my out-of-office automatic response, hit "save," shut down my computer, and walked out. In my mind, I already knew I wasn't going to return to work until I felt better. What would happen to the organization until that time was still unknown.

A few days later, during meditation, an image of a blazing fire flashed across my mind. I knew it represented where I was in my life. In order to get to where I wanted to go, I was first going to have to walk through this fire and take accountability for how I'd ended up there to begin with.

When I got to California, I headed to the hotel room I was sharing with my friend and got ready for the wedding. We hopped in a cab and got out at a Beverly Hills mansion. I took a specialty cocktail and waited with the rest of Jennifer's friends for the wedding to start.

It was hard not to compare my life to hers that day. I wasn't anywhere close to where I wanted to be. Jennifer was about to have this beautiful celebration with people she loved, and I couldn't even pay cash for the dress I was wearing to the wedding. I was a month from turning thirty-five, and my life was so uncomfortable. To turn my mind off, I leaned back in my chair and scrolled through a social media app.

Jennifer's photo was the first image that caught my eye. It was a picture of her shoes and a little bit of her wedding dress with a cute little saying about coming down the aisle to meet her man. I laughed and felt a bubble of love fill me up. I held on to that all day.

Later that night, I felt such joy for my girlfriend and the love of her life on their magical, heartfelt day surrounded by all their favorite people. And for the first time in a long time, I could breathe a little deeper.

I flew back to Phoenix for a few days, slept through most of them, and got back on a plane for Nashville to meet my friend Celeste for her special weekend. I texted her as soon as I landed, and we met in the airport lobby. We hugged, laughed, and even cried a little bit out of pure joy at seeing each other.

Nashville was everything I needed it to be. It was a blank canvas where I didn't have to talk about my life or my lack of funds. I listened to music, hugged my friends, took in the sounds and sights, and met new people. I danced, drank—a lot—did the Nashville thing with one of my favorite women. And I loved it.

When I got back to Phoenix, there was a check in the mail from USA Network. I had been selected as a 2013 Characters Unite Award winner. It was a huge honor, and a major milestone in my life. Every year, the campaign highlighted people around the country who had made strides to combat hate and discrimination. In 2013, I was one of those people.

I had known the donation was coming; I just hadn't known when. I held the check in my hands in my kitchen late one Sunday night and couldn't get myself to open it. I knew the check inside was my saving grace. I knew it was for $5,000, and while I was so grateful for it, I also resented it. That check would be the largest dollar amount I would have personally received since launching the business. And I couldn't even keep all of it because I had to pay insurance for the organization. I was so tired and knew that if I really allowed myself to feel what I needed to feel, I'd have a meltdown on my kitchen floor. I was too fatigued for all that mess. So I folded the envelope in half, placed it in my wallet, and went to bed.

The next day I did my laundry, repacked for Wisconsin, and went to the bank. I took the envelope out of my wallet, opened it, and turned it over before even looking at the amount. I just wanted to get to Wisconsin before I unraveled. I signed my name on the back of the $5,000 check and deposited it into the Severson Sisters account. I sent off a check to the insurance company and gave the rest to myself as a paycheck. The next morning, I left for Wisconsin.

When I boarded the plane that day, I really didn't expect to come back to Severson Sisters. I was finished. I resented the work. I resented the organization. I didn't want to fight anymore. And I was just fine with that. What would happen to it was something I couldn't yet see. I had succeeded in doing what I'd said I was going to do. I'd created an organization, and we'd been successful in terms of the number of lives we had impacted. But I didn't feel attached to the person who'd had that success. I felt like a failure inside. I didn't feel supported. I didn't feel strong. I didn't feel whole.

I woke up the day after I'd arrived at my childhood home in Wisconsin ready to start a new life. At least, that's what I told myself. I turned off my phone, placed it in the kitchen junk drawer, and kept my computer on a high shelf in my closet so it was out of sight. I knew the only way I was going to understand how to change my life was to be still and clear the clutter from my head. I knew it was going to be hard, and I knew that as soon as I started it, I'd be different. Change was what I craved the most.

I really wanted to start this process, jump into the firepit, and run through the flames. I realized, though, that was my problem. My problem was my fight-or-flight mechanism. It created this race against time. But time meant nothing there in Wisconsin. My agenda for the day included watching the clouds and listening to the birds. That was it. Time had nothing to do with that.

I, on the other hand, couldn't help but force this process to start. I didn't know how to just lean back and let it unfold at its own pace. I'd been running my whole life. I couldn't hear or feel past the present moment, which I guess meant I was in a state of relaxation. I just hadn't realized it at the time. I was so sure I was supposed to be fighting my way through it as I had with everything else in life. I was so sure I was supposed to cry, scream, swear, and some sort of healing would happen. Instead, all I felt was peace.

Chapter Six

THE BURNOUT

A S MY DAYS IN WISCONSIN WENT BY, I WAITED FOR THE AHA
moments to take place. I thought if I just stopped working, I'd
feel lighter and better. That wasn't the case. Every morning I'd splash
water on face, make a strong cup of coffee, and sit on the back porch.
The pine trees that my parents had planted when we moved into the
house in 1989 provided a prickly green shield from the surrounding
neighbors. I dragged one of the deck chairs into a patch of shade on
the corner of the deck. The white plastic of the chair was stained
from twenty years of summer, and dead leaves covered the padding.
I shook off the leaves and sat down, half expecting the plastic to
crack underneath me. I extended my legs onto a bench in front of
me and leaned my head back to watch the clouds for a minute.

I inhaled as much of the early-summer air as I could and held my breath.

I sat on the leaf-crusted, twenty-year-old patio chair drinking coffee, listening to birds, and watching clouds roll by. I was ready to dig in. I just had no idea how to start. I had my pen in hand, ready to write, but couldn't find a single word. So instead, I wrote down what I loved about my childhood home:

The wallpaper.
The sunroom.
My closet.
The fireplace.

I paused to take a sip of coffee. I scanned my surroundings and made a mental note of all the different flowers and colors around me. The morning was perfect, and my next exhale was so big that my shoulders dropped and I felt more settled into the cushion.

Finally, an idea came to mind.

What if I write down all the feelings I have right now and why I have them?

I picked up my pen and started writing. Hours went by. I'd stop to refill my coffee, grab something to eat, and brush my teeth, but that was it. I was onto something and wanted to capture every thought in my journal as each emotional flavor popped up. I questioned everything. An emotion led to a question, which then brought up a brand-new emotion.

It looked like this:

Resentment—*I resent how much of my life is taken up by my job.*

What would my life look like without resentment? Light. Why do I feel I have to work so hard? To raise money.

Suffocation—*I can't take deep breaths because I can't pay my bills.*

What would happen if I got a part-time job to pay my bills? I wouldn't be able to do as much for Severson Sisters or for the girls.

Guilt—*I feel guilty that I can't pay my own bills doing what I feel I'm supposed to do with my life.*

At what point will it be okay to take care of myself? I'm past that point. I am committed to taking care of myself.

Is there anything wrong with taking care of myself? No.

Am I ready to stop feeling guilty? YES!

Exhaustion—*I'm so tired and anxiety ridden.*

What would happen if I were rested and at peace? I'd be balanced and healthy.

Balanced and Healthy—*I'm out of balance and unhealthy because I'm working too hard and emotionally drained. I'm willing to change my cycle of lack.*

What would happen if my cycle of lack changed? I'd be happy.

Happy—I love my job, and it does bring me great joy. I'm missing personal happiness, though, and that's what I'm craving.

What does personal happiness look like? Love. Fun. Light. Ease. Grace. Feminine.

Feminine—I want to love my body and myself again. Feel pretty. Be present in my life again. Receive. Feel worthy. Feel supported.

How do I get that? Slow down. Dance to music again. Explore. Hike. Do my nails. Go out with friends. See a doctor for help with my body. Ask for help. Use money from my birthday to start going to Pilates again.

With each emotional aspect that showed up on the page, the feeling of the emotion itself swelled inside me. The bitterness of feeling resentful and exhausted for so long weighed on my shoulders. The lack of happiness and feeling feminine knotted itself up in my belly.

As I ran through the emotions and feelings, I sobbed. I screamed. I stomped my feet. I'm sure there were neighbors concerned that something crazy was happening at the Severson house. I didn't care. I just kept going. I knew I had to let all this stuff out to get to the other side.

The time came for me to stop and process everything that had just come up. I took a shower, curled up on the couch, and fell asleep.

That writing session was so intense. It took a lot out of me. I didn't move the rest of the day and crawled into my bed early that night.

The next morning I was emotionally exhausted, but I felt relieved, like I had taken off a weighted vest. Before I left my bedroom that morning, I noticed a stack of journals I had brought back to Wisconsin from Arizona on the corner of my dresser. I grabbed them and headed downstairs.

I took a seat on the back porch with my coffee and journals. I spent some time listening to the birds, admiring my mom's flower bed, and paying attention to how the breeze felt on my skin.

Without really thinking about it, I opened one of the journals. I mindlessly started reading the thoughts captured on the page from earlier in the year. Already, the change within me was apparent. I read through entry after entry and could clearly see the struggle and despair. I had deep empathy for the woman I was on those pages.

Soon, a pattern caught my eye.

I noticed the same four words appeared on many pages.

Enough.

Need.

Want.

Busy.

I circled them to make sure my eyes weren't playing tricks on me.

One word popped off the pages like a 3D image.

Enough.

I had tossed it around like confetti in my daily journal entries. There was never *enough*. I wasn't *enough*. I didn't have *enough* time. We didn't have *enough* money. We didn't have *enough* people on the board or working in the organization. I would show gratitude for a check that came in that was *enough* to cover a bill. And then I'd say something similar the next day. And the day after that. All I manifested was a financial flow just strong *enough* to cover what I needed covered. And my head was so far underwater that I couldn't think about anything but the pain of trying to stay above water, to reach that level of *enough*.

Enough was poison for my mental health.

It left a deep wound in my stomach.

Intuitively I knew there was more healing I had to do around this one word. I just wasn't ready for it yet. I vowed to delete the word from my vocabulary.

Looking back at that moment, the simple act of not using the word was just a Band-Aid. The deep healing around accepting myself as *enough* came eight years later.

A month after I had gone back to Wisconsin, I began to feel lighter. I found a clearing, and I was running toward it with some confidence.

I had checked my phone a few times over the course of a month and had a few touch points with each board member. Nothing important was pressing, and everyone was fine with me staying away a bit longer.

Chapter Seven

HAPPY BIRTHDAY

I ROLLED OVER ONTO MY RIGHT SIDE AND JAMMED MY HANDS under my pillow. With my eyes still shut, I went through the day's to-do list.

Say thank you.
Open gifts.
Bloody Marys.
Brewery tour.
Dinner with family.
Eat cake.

I contracted my legs, wiggled my toes, circled my ankles, and inhaled as deeply as I could. My joints crackled and popped. I pressed myself farther into my mattress and exhaled.

A word flashed across my mind: *burnout*.

I wasn't surprised. Random words or thoughts often came to mind first thing in the morning, and those random morning messages typically served me well. It's why I'd named the nonprofit Severson Sisters. It's why we'd named the program Super Girl. And that day, it was why I researched the word *burnout*.

The door to my parents' bedroom squeaked open and clicked shut. The footsteps on the staircase sounded like my dad's.

I opened my eyes and glared at the clock on the nightstand: *6:45 a.m.*

I wrestled with the sheets for a few seconds and then reached over to the nightstand and turned on my phone. I waited for the screen to change colors and come to life. When it did, I tapped in my password and was notified that I had twenty-five new voice mails, 12,543 e-mails, and twenty-nine birthday text messages.

I opened up a browser, typed in the word *burnout*, and clicked the magnifying glass. Pages and pages of psychology articles popped up. I clicked on one article after another, reading the first few paragraphs and then moving on.

A lump formed in my throat, my eyes blurred with tears, and snot formed at the edge of my nostrils. I exhaled hard and squeezed my eyelids shut. Tears slid down my cheeks and pooled at my earlobe. I rolled onto my back, put my phone down, and said it out loud.

"Burnout."

The pages and pages of articles I read all said the same thing. Burnout was real caused by chronic stress. People who experienced burnout reported having long-term exhaustion and diminished interest in their work and sometimes their personal life.

I finally had a word to describe what I was experiencing. *Burnout.*

That was it. A single, thirty-five-year-old entrepreneur who suffered from extreme exhaustion.

I took a deep breath but couldn't move the air past my chest. A panic attack was coming on. I put one hand on my heart and the other on my belly, and focused on my breathing. It was impossible to fight back the tears so I just let them come.

Heartbeat. Breath. Safe. Secure. Supported. Loved.

Heartbeat. Breath. Safe. Secure. Supported. Loved.

Heartbeat. Breath. Safe. Secure. Supported. Loved.

Once my panic attack ran its course, I rubbed my eyes with the palms of my hands and sat up. I ran my hands over my cheeks and down my neck, wiping the tears off my skin. I looked down at my breasts pouring out over my nightgown, and my stomach that protruded farther than I wanted it to. The fifty pounds that my body had packed on over the course of the last three years were everywhere. *Everywhere.* I couldn't avoid them. I couldn't get rid of them, either.

I knew why the weight had come on. I'd created a nonprofit for girls and had run at a speed I hadn't known existed. I'd run out of money too many times to count, resulting in either buying the cheapest and poorest quality food to fuel my body or simply accepting, with so much gratitude, whatever food people brought me. My thyroid and adrenal glands had both quit on me. I was tired and depressed.

I glanced up at myself in the bedroom mirror across from my bed and tried to recognize myself. When I was a little girl, I'd look at myself in the same mirror and make promises to myself.

We're going to change the world.

We're not going to get married until we become a boss of something.

We're going to have the best husband around, and he's going to love us.

We're going to be a great mom and raise two kids.

I craved companionship and happiness and ease and love and health. And I had no idea where to find any of them.

"Hello, Carrie," I said quietly. "Your birthday gift to yourself is to accept yourself as a burnout. You're a burnout, and that's okay. Everything will get better now."

I didn't feel okay. I didn't look okay. I was so far beyond the point of being okay. But accepting myself as a burnout was the only thing I hadn't tried yet. It had to work.

Birthdays are a big deal in my family. We get flowers and have a jam-packed day of activities. There are three-foot-tall cards and tons of food and an embarrassing chorus of "Happy Birthday to You."

My sister was visiting our childhood home at the same time I was, and our parents were in the house, as well. I knew my dad was up, but I couldn't hear him anymore. I had to make it across the house to a bathroom so I could wash away all signs of tears before anyone saw me. My mom always knew when I had been crying, and I didn't want to talk about it. I never wanted to talk about it.

I swung my legs over my bed and slowly stood up, trying not to make a sound. I raised myself up onto the balls of my feet and took several steps forward.

I pressed my ear to my bedroom door and waited. It was still. It was silent. Nobody was in the hallway. The door was oak and had a habit of sticking in the summer, so I put one hand against the doorjamb and the other on the door, and pulled it open in one smooth movement.

I stood in my doorway with my hands still in place. It took me a few seconds to register the Happy Birthday banner and streamers hanging from the ceiling and the red, blue, yellow, and green balloons covering the hallway floor.

I concentrated on the words *Happy Birthday* dangling in front of me. Both words hit me but for different reasons. This day was a milestone for me. It wasn't just my thirty-fifth birthday. This day would mark the day I accepted myself as a burnout. It'd be an anniversary for years to come. This was my turning point. And I had balloons and streamers and a banner to celebrate the occasion. I could be happy. I knew how to do that. I had felt that within the last month. It wasn't too far under the surface.

I can do that, I thought.

I could feel the corners of my lips turn upward. A laugh formed in my belly and jiggled its way up my torso. I covered my mouth and stifled the laugh with my fingers because I still wasn't ready to see anyone else just yet.

I kicked my way through the sea of balloons in the hallway to the bathroom, noticing the way they bounced off the floor.

Ten red balloons.

Ten yellow balloons.

Ten blue balloons.

Five green balloons.

I bent over the bathroom sink and filled my hands with cold water. I lowered my face into my hands to let the icy water shock my capillaries and pores awake. I did it again. And again. The more I did it, the clearer I could think. So I did it again. And again. And again. By the twentieth time, I was laughing. I kept going. By the thirty-fifth shock, the top of my nightgown and the crown of my head were soaked.

I dabbed my face with a hand towel and smiled at myself in the mirror.

"You'll be okay," I said.

I sopped up the water around the sink and on the floor with the hand towel and hung it above the toilet. I tiptoed back out into the hallway and snuck downstairs, skipping the second squeaky step from the top. I made my way into the kitchen and turned on the lights. Yellow, blue, red, and green balloons lined the ceiling, and bright-pink bouquets of flowers lined the kitchen counter.

I inhaled as deeply as I could to take it all in. I held my breath in my chest for a few seconds and exhaled slowly.

While I waited for the coffee machine to heat up, I looked through a cupboard in the kitchen that was always filled with craft supplies. The creative components of the nonprofit seeped into everyone's home, my parents' place in Wisconsin included. I found glue, scissors, and a sketch pad with blank pages. I placed them on the kitchen table and went to search for the stack of magazines I'd bought at the airport but hadn't read on the plane. I found them on a table in the next room and added them to the pile of craft materials on the kitchen table.

I grabbed the largest coffee cup in the cupboard and the darkest coffee option in the lazy Susan, and I made myself a cup of coffee.

I sat down at the kitchen table. Typically, I started my day with a letter to the Universe. The letter usually had daily intentions and requests, things I was grateful for and questions I wanted answers to. Writing a letter to the Universe wasn't something I wanted to do that day, though. Instead, I sat there at the kitchen table, alone. The silence was heavy, and I could feel it weighing on me.

I looked around the room at all the birthday decorations. I was loved. I was safe. I was supported. It didn't matter that I was broke and alone and felt ashamed of my financial situation and emotional burnout.

I took a long drink from my coffee cup and set it aside. I was thirty-five, and that day, I was going to pretend my life was everything I wanted it to be.

That day, I was rich in all ways.

That day, I was in a beautiful partnership with myself.

That day, I knew God had my back.

That day, I had this great man waiting to wish me "Happy Birthday" at any moment.

That day, I had friends all over the place who knew what I was really going through.

That day, I was healthy.

That day, I was connected to my body.

That day, I was successful.

That day, I was at peace.

That day, life was perfect.

I sat at the kitchen table, in the same chair I sat in every night as a child, staring at the pine trees in the backyard. I watched the sparrows invade the bird feeder as I finished my first cup of coffee. I closed my eyes and let the sound of the birds and the nearby wind chime carry me off somewhere new.

I looked down at the table and the pile of magazines and crafting supplies I needed to make a vision board.

I knew enough about how manifestation worked to know that in order to move past the point I was at, I had to do something new. I had to believe something new. I had to create positive intentions for myself and a visual to focus on.

Words have obviously been my thing since declaring journalism as my major in college, but the idea of visualization had helped me since becoming an entrepreneur, despite the fact that I didn't feel like a good one.

I thought back to that night on the floor with Ellie Mae. We were surrounded by images I tore out of magazines. That night inspired me to create Severson Sisters. If I could do it once, I could do it again.

I looked at all the birthday decorations and felt a surge of gratitude swell up in my heart. I took several deep breaths and with each exhale gave so much gratitude to my family for loving me that much. They wanted me to be happy.

As I continued with my breathing exercise, I let my mind wander about the things that made me happy. Words popped into my mind.

Love
Travel
Peace
Health
Fun
Adventure
Compassion
Friendship

I was inspired. I flipped through magazines and tore out images that resonated with words like *love, adventure,* and *friendship.* This was the new me and this new way of life I wanted to create. It didn't take long. After I pulled them out of the magazines, I glued them to the piece of sketch paper.

It was a new year. I was going to start fresh. I was going to dream up new dreams all year long and fall in love with myself, and hopefully somebody else. I was going to write again and be nice to myself again. Most importantly, I was going to learn how to be at peace each day, create new friendships, and have some adventure. I knew I wanted romantic love, but even as I promised to open my heart, I first had to love myself again. I had no idea what that adventure would be like for me, but when that word came to mind, I trusted that it would serve me in great ways.

That was the kind of life I wanted. That was the kind of woman I had always set out to be. But somewhere between launching Severson Sisters and turning thirty-five, I had lost my way. I leaned back in my chair, held my now-cold cup of coffee in my hands, and studied my 2013 vision board.

I turned the piece of sketch paper over and started writing.

July 17, 2013—A 365-Day Contract

I, Carrie Severson, swear to put myself first for the next year. I promise to ask for help. I promise to say no when I need to. I promise to acknowledge my emotions, limits, and abilities. I promise to find myself. I promise to get healthy. I promise to open my heart. I promise to let more people know me. I promise to have fun again. I promise to make my life an adventure that I enjoy being on again. I promise to really stay open to my soul's purpose and spend time searching for the true meaning of my life. I promise to never end up here in this burnout wasteland again.

Carrie Severson

I was nowhere near understanding what I was really promising myself with that contract, but I had to start somewhere.

My sister crept into the kitchen, smiling. She looked innocent and sweet, and I soaked it in. I put my soul quest on pause for the day; I'd walk through the fire tomorrow. Or at least I'd hang out by it with a marshmallow and some chocolate. Walking through it might not happen for a while.

That day was the day I'd agreed to wake up. I didn't just want to feel better, get healthier, and ditch all the debt and doubt that came with chasing that void for so long. I wanted to feel soulfully aligned with my own greatest good.

And my soul quest to meet a new Carrie started.

I leaned back again and closed my eyes. I whispered a final prayer to God and asked for guidance on how to start this process.

And the word *boundaries* came to mind.

Chapter Eight

CREATING BOUNDARIES

WHENEVER A WORD SUDDENLY CAME TO MIND AFTER A MEDitation, prayer, or journaling exercise, I knew it was important. So when *boundaries* flashed in my brain after journaling on my thirty-fifth birthday, I took notice.

Creating boundaries had always seemed like a daunting, nerve-racking, totally intense, grown-up thing to do. And at that point in my life, I sucked at it. Prior to my burnout, boundaries had only worked with exes—and they hadn't even really worked then, considering I usually ended up just finding new places to hang out and blocking the guy on my phone.

Since I was never really successful with boundaries before, I spent the next few weeks reading as much as I could about "healthy boundaries."

Boundaries became my theme for the second part of 2013. The biggest boundary I created was around my dedication to staying in a happy, peaceful bubble. I knew I needed time to do things that lifted my spirits every day.

Before I bought a ticket back to Phoenix, I set a few new boundaries.

After two months of being out of the office, I grew to like not being so available. I deleted my e-mail and all the social media apps from my phone and gave myself permission to keep them off my phone for the next quarter.

My calendar was next. I blocked out the first two hours of each day for meditation, journaling, and exercise. Nobody could ever book a meeting with me before 10:00 a.m.

After a quick internet search, I found a two-week coupon to a dance studio and downloaded their calendar. I scheduled dance classes for the first two weeks after landing back in Phoenix.

Finally, I forced myself to buy a one-way ticket back to Phoenix in August 2013. I wasn't totally healed or even ready to work again, but I felt better since taking the time to lean into what boundaries meant to me and how they needed to factor into my new life.

While on the plane from Wisconsin to Arizona, I also made a list of twenty nonnegotiables I needed to incorporate in my new life. These twenty things would help me find my new voice, unapologetically claim it, express it, own it, live it, love it, and move forward in it.

1. Fun
2. Playtime
3. Meditation
4. Journaling

5.	Friends	13.	Creation time
6.	Writing	14.	Support
7.	Dancing	15.	Church
8.	Walking on grass	16.	Spirituality
9.	The ocean	17.	High-quality food
10.	Traveling	18.	Massages
11.	Money	19.	Family time
12.	Romance	20.	Naturopathic care

Boundaries had to go in and around each and every one of those twenty elements. I stared at my list of nonnegotiables and made a promise to myself that this list was going to change my life. I was certain that I could reorganize my life to include these twenty elements.

After unpacking my life in Phoenix, I hung my new vision board in my bedroom. Knowing my birthday contract was on the back, I vowed up and down and pinkie swore that I wouldn't even flirt with the idea of burnout. I'd always know where my burnout line was now, and when it got too close, I'd run the other way. It sounded like a fantastic plan to me!

Figuring out how to do it, on the other hand, caused me some anxiety. I kept going back and forth between feeling guilty for wanting to set boundaries and feeling lazy for not working harder.

During the first few weeks home, I learned how to speak to myself the way I would speak to a friend. I went easy on the trash talk in my head, and when I recognized I was trash-talking myself, I snapped my fingers and said something positive about myself.

I'm a smart woman.

I'm an intelligent woman.

I created something for the greatest good of lots of souls.
I follow my heart.
I know what I'm doing.
I have faith in myself.

I kept finding positive things to say about myself until I felt lighter, brighter, better.

After a week or so, I called a meeting of the Severson Sisters board of directors for what felt like an intervention. I was the one talking about the necessary changes we all had to make as an organization.

I used the F-word a lot that day. In addition to the big, fat F-word, I did let them know how disappointed I was with each of them for standing on the sidelines while I caught on fire and flamed out. Their job as board members—especially as board members of a young nonprofit—was to jump in and help keep the organization afloat and thriving. I apologized for putting them in such a demanding position and gave them the opportunity to step down right then and there, no questions asked. One board member did. The others stayed on, and we moved forward.

Everything about Severson Sisters had to change. I wasn't going to go back to burnout ever again. It was a heavy, dark place that I didn't fully understand, but I knew there was no way I'd survive it again.

That day, we decided to create a new way of supporting young girls through our program. Super Girl could no longer happen with just me and a few volunteers. My soul craved more support, and I was no longer going to pile up my car with art supplies and workbooks, and drive from point A to point B for pennies. We decided to create a Train-the-Trainer program and license our program and curriculum to individuals who wanted to be Severson Sisters Super Girl facilitators.

How we would do that was something I was willing to figure out over the course of the next several months. We decided to launch this new way of doing business in January 2014 at a party thrown in my honor in recognition of the Characters Unite award I'd won. That meant I had five months to ease my way back into the business and figure out how to run it.

Just that little shift created space in my life to explore. I felt as though I split my day with Severson Sisters at first. That in itself brought on an interesting challenge. I was still the heart of the organization, and yet I was simultaneously working through my resentment of how it had run my life for years. Hence the boundaries I needed to set. I had to continue to serve the organization for its greater good and, at the same time, honor *my* greater good.

I was determined to stick to my boundaries, and each day I decided how much I was going to work, and then I'd work on just a few projects. When my pre-set hours were over, I would turn off my computer, no matter where I was in a project. It wasn't easy at first. I had a lot of self-judgment around being lazy or slacking off. Still, I walked away from work when I was supposed to.

During this new phase of my life, I found that I had to change my destination a lot. I'd work in a certain space until the energy there no longer inspired me. I'd stay there as long as I felt good. If I felt any heaviness in my body at all, I'd find a new place to work, read, write, and socialize. I went through a major chain and three local coffee shops over the next handful of months.

Mountains that I used to hike while looking and hoping for clarity made me sick to my stomach after my thirty-fifth birthday. I found a new mountain, and instead of hiking it, I would sit and meditate on a rock in the middle of nowhere.

My next boundary had to do with fun. I missed having fun! So I had to do something fun for myself at least once a week. It didn't have to cost money. It just had to be consistent.

That was easy.

Reading books before bed.

Watching an old movie and laughing super hard.

Going swimming.

Coloring.

Painting.

By the time January 2014 came around, I had more clarity and felt much lighter. I was well on my way to being happy. I felt more grounded than I had since starting Severson Sisters and taking the leap of faith to blindly follow my purpose with my passion. I had done the work to move Severson Sisters into a position to license our Super Girl program out to individuals. I had hired a trainer, and we had scheduled trips to California, New York, and Wisconsin to train facilitators.

I spent all of March and some of April 2014 in Wisconsin. I worked and played and found some really great balance there. I stayed at my childhood home the entire time to save the organization money. I drove their car, worked from my dad's office building, and came and went as I pleased. To bring Severson

Sisters to Wisconsin was surreal, and to be in a place where I could see straight and bring our Super Girl program to the city where I had grown up felt right. I connected with old friends while I was back in Wisconsin, too, and rekindled old relationships I missed.

Over the course of the next several months, the fog and mud faded. As I continued to set boundaries for myself on my soul quest, I felt healthier.

The more I leaned back and allowed myself to take this soul quest, the better the organization did financially, as well. I was being supported. I could pay bills again. And I rarely worried about affording groceries. By June of that year, I felt comfortable in my own skin again. I hadn't lost any of the weight I'd put on, but my thyroid and adrenal glands were being supported again, thanks to the naturopathic team I could afford to work with.

One full year had passed since I'd learned how to stop running and started learning how to feed into my intuitive energy and my soul's journey back to happiness. I had relationships again, and my behavior with money definitely shifted after burnout. I would spend money on experiences and the parts of life that would keep my spirits up. I kept flowers in the house every week. I could afford to drive across town to see friends. I could purchase birthday gifts again. I even felt like connecting with new people.

When my thirty-sixth birthday rolled around in July 2014, I was even ready to start dating again!

I craved romantic love and knew I had to go through a layer of my soul quest to self-love first. I decided to begin networking for fun, and I did what came naturally to me. I looked into writing groups and came full circle.

I came out of burnout with a deeper understanding of who I am, refreshed, whole, and appreciative of all I had to go through to accept myself as unapologetically enough. My soul quest had led me back to one of my first loves—writing. I felt comfortable being vulnerable again. I felt whole again. It was working. And people noticed.

My friend Jessica asked me to take care of her cats while she went on vacation in the fall of 2014. She lived in Santa Monica, and I jumped at the chance to spend a few weeks by the beach. While I was there, I received an invitation to a dinner party at a new friend's house. New connections were something I was still craving so I instantly accepted.

While at dinner that night, I learned of a club for women writers. I jumped right into the new network of writers and introduced myself as a "recovering burnout."

Later that week, I applied to be a blogger with the Huffington Post. My first blog post with the Huffington Post was called "I'm A Recovering Burnout." It was published on a Friday, and by the following Tuesday, hundreds and hundreds of women—and one man—had reached out to me to thank me for putting a name to what they were personally experiencing.

Burnout.

I wasn't alone. They weren't alone, either.

I sat in my living room for days e-mailing with strangers. I felt connected and seen.

Suddenly, I realized why I had gone through what I had.

If I had found a way past the clutter of my own mind and trail blazed a way to uncover my own unique truth without professional accolades, a life partner, or children, then other women could see it for themselves, too.

I am a vessel for stories. My soul quest to waking up to my own divine, unapologetic self could help others do the same. I just had to write it all down and get it out into the world.

Part II

AN UNAPOLOGETIC VOICE ON LOVE

Chapter Nine

FINDING A NEW GROOVE

AFTER I FOUND A NEW GROOVE IN MY WRITING AND STARTED publicly sharing my burnout story, I set clear intentions to be open and welcome intimate conversations and connections. And since I knew my life was in the hands of a higher power, I set intentions for these conversations and connections to lead me to men I wanted to date.

In June 2014, I met my friend Maggie. Maggie is a magical, spiritual, spunky woman, and for many years, I called her my fairy godmother.

She and I connected right away. There was something about her that made me listen harder. I leaned in just to get closer to her energy. As it turned out, she felt the same way about me.

One of the first things she ever said to me was "I get you."

How brilliant, I thought. I loved that! She got me—not what I did for a living or my mission in life, just me!

Our friendship evolved over the course of the first year I knew her, and over the course of that year, she'd spent more time asking me about my love life than anything else. So I wasn't surprised when she asked me to her house for lunch one day to talk about men.

Lunch at Maggie's house was a half-day production. We made Greek salad, tilapia, and key lime pie. She set out a tablecloth, candles, and her good china for just us two. It totally felt like we were on a date!

The energy in the room changed a bit when we sat down. Maggie bowed her head, whispered something to herself, and said, "Amen."

I closed my eyes and said *Amen* to myself.

Maggie dug into lunch and moaned and congratulated us on a job well done.

We ate in silence, which was unusual to me. We had already been together for hours and Maggie had asked me every question she could about my life and what I wanted to manifest in life and in a soul mate. I figured we were talked out and a silent lunch was appropriate.

And then suddenly Maggie slammed her hands down on the table, stood up, and ran out of the kitchen screaming, "I can't believe I hadn't thought of him before!"

I wanted to ask her what was going on but I was practically choking on tilapia.

She was still talking about this man that had popped into her head when she came back into the room with her laptop. She opened it up, wiped her fingers on her napkin, and double-clicked the mouse.

"I'm sending a message to my friend Ruby," Maggie said. *"Dear Ruby, I know your son's soul mate. Please call me. Love Maggie."*

She shut her laptop and went back to eating.

Meanwhile, across the table, I waited for her to look up at me and explain what had just happened. I had fish on my fork, my napkin clenched in my other hand, and a peppercorn stuck in my teeth. I ran my tongue back and forth against it as I thought about what to say next. After a few moments, I asked, "Maggie, was that about me?"

She nodded, not looking at me. She kept eating.

I put my fork down and dabbed my mouth with my napkin. I took a long drink of wine and leaned back in my chair. I finally said, "Can we talk about Ruby and her son?"

"You'll love him. I think his name is Rick," Maggie said.

My eyes were a few sizes bigger at this point. I leaned in a little bit and touched her arm. "Maggie? You *think* his name is Rick?"

"Yeah, you'll love him," Maggie said, grinning.

I leaned back and smiled. "Okay, what's he like?"

"He's passionate and really smart and just a great guy. You'll love him."

"Yeah, you've said that." I laughed because, at this point, I had to. "What does Rick do?"

"He's a photographer," Maggie said.

And then she said, "I think he is a photographer."

Our lunch ended without me learning anything new about my so-called soul mate. I helped clean up Maggie's kitchen, and before I left, I accepted an invite back to her house the following night for a dinner party she was having.

The next morning, I wrote a letter to the Universe and thanked it for Maggie's magic in my life. I promised to let it lead me wherever it wanted to, and then I meditated for a bit and went to work.

The first e-mail I got that Friday was from Maggie. The subject line was *I love the way the Universe works.*

> *Carrie,*
>
> *Wear lipstick tonight. Ruby is coming to dinner tonight to meet you.*
>
> > *Love,*
> > *Maggie*
>
> *P.S. His name is really Matt.*

I responded to Maggie with this:

> *Good morning, Magical Maggie!*
>
> *I love the way the Universe works, too. See you soon!*
>
> > *Love,*
> > *Carrie*

I was really surprised at how comfortable I was throughout the day. I didn't feel anxious or worried. There was no trash talk or what-ifs going on in my head. I was really impressed with myself!

That all changed when I got in the car to head to Maggie's house for dinner. She lived thirty minutes from me so I had plenty of time to freak out on the way there, but it didn't feel *weird* until I parked the car and got to the front door.

Maggie met me, hugged me, and gave me a kiss on the cheek. She whispered in my ear that she loved the shade of red I was wearing on my lips, and then she grabbed my hand and led me inside.

Matt's mother was waiting for me there.

"Ruby, this is the young lady I told you about," Maggie said.

I introduced myself and shifted my weight awkwardly. I'm a hugger, but my intuitive guidance system told me not to hug Ruby. I held out my hand, and Ruby very lightly shook it. She was very formal and put together. Every hair was in place, and her makeup looked professionally applied. After we shook hands, she sat back down at the kitchen island where her glass of champagne was waiting. She motioned for me to take a seat next to her.

I was prepared to answer the usual questions from women Ruby's age:

What do I do?
Have I ever been married before?
Why not?
Do I want children?

Instead, Ruby and I talked about everything else: my upbringing, family, Maggie, dinner, the town we lived in, and the places we grew up. My love life never came up. And after a while, I forgot that I was there because our shared friend assumed I was a good fit for Ruby's son. We shared a lovely bottle of champagne and enjoyed each other's company. It felt really natural.

Nothing ever manifested with Matt and me outside of that night, but the encounter gave me hope that something magical could happen in my life.

The day after Maggie's dinner party, I was happy and content with my life. I felt like I had fulfilled my thirty-fifth-birthday contract. I had found some peace, balance, fun, and adventure in my life. And I felt as if I had finally opened my heart.

In the months to follow, whenever I was asked about my love life, I'd respond by saying, "I'm available and taking applications!"

I encouraged friends to set me up on dates and joined a dating website one night over a bottle of wine with a girlfriend. I said yes to every man who asked me out.

I dated many men that next year and had great dates, good dates, and really bad dates. I learned a lot about what I really wanted in a lifelong partner.

By the time I was thirty-seven, I had found that most men wanted to know why I hadn't been married before. It was the question I was asked more than any other.

This was the case with Jay, a forty-eight-year-old divorced man with two children. On our fourth date, he invited me over to his home for spaghetti. We were deep into our interview process at this point in the game.

After dinner, he poured me a little Frangelico for dessert and asked me to join him on the couch. I curled up in the corner, and he sat next to me, patted my thigh, and said it.

"So why haven't you been married before?"

I smiled and went into the answer I gave most men. "I wanted to create something outside a relationship first. I guess I needed to gain more life experience before being open to a relationship."

Jay looked at me, still with his hand on my thigh, and said, "It's a shame you missed your window of opportunity to get married. And you know, honey, if you don't have children within the next year, you'll miss your opportunity there, too."

His comment hung in front of me like fog.

What do I do now? Did he really just say that? Where's my purse?

I calmly stood. "I have Pilates in the morning so I'm going to go home now."

I kept my eyes on his front door as I moved from room to room. Jay was a few steps behind me, talking about seeing me again. I stopped when I reached the front door and faced him. I thought about telling him how insulted I was or that I've always seen myself as a wife and mom, but instead, I just walked out.

I thought of all the single women my age and older who were still hopeful that our people were out there looking for us. I thought about all the women my age and older who had given up on love because they were over the dating game. I thought of my grandma, who'd had her youngest child days before she turned forty-two.

The next morning, I told my friends in Pilates about my date. They were outraged, which actually helped me move past being insulted and take back my own power.

Later that day, Jay sent a text to ask if I was available for dinner the following evening. I considered calling him to end it altogether. In my heart, though, I knew this was an opportunity to tell Jay he was wrong about the millions of women like me.

Jay took me out for pizza, and before he dished up the first slice, I told him that what I've done with my life wasn't something he could define as a missed opportunity. I told him that his placing time restraints on my life was inappropriate.

"I'll meet my man one day, and we'll raise children," I said. "I'm not worried about when I become a wife or how I become a mom."

I talked about all the women out there who were available for partnership and motherhood. We were dating younger men, older men, divorced men, single dads, college-educated men, and those who went right into the workforce after high school. Not all of us were dating to get married and have children, but I was.

Jay mumbled something as a response, but I just shrugged him off and thanked him for listening to me. Though, really, I was grateful I had been able stand up for myself out loud in a way I hadn't before.

For his part, Jay remained calm and unaffected. He stated that he knew women who had babies at my age were considered high-risk and that the babies had a higher chance of being born with abnormalities. After that, he was ready to move on to the next topic.

And then he invited me back to his house.

I declined.

I woke up the next morning a little depressed. I questioned how many more men like Jay I was going to have to date and defend my life path to. I let that daunting question *Where is my man?* sneak in. And for the first time in a long time, I also wondered if I would ever know what motherhood was like.

Both my siblings had married in their twenties. Both had birthed children in their twenties. Marriage and motherhood were always dreams of mine, but after my month-long experience with Jay, I felt a little deflated.

I was well aware that it was harder, but still not impossible, for me to have children myself since I was already in my late thirties. I let that feeling linger for most of the morning and then remembered my burnout contract.

I jumped off the couch to get my journal, then ripped a piece of paper out and grabbed a pen. I stared at the paper for a long time. I could feel the tears burning up inside, but I refused to let them fall. I felt the need to hold them in while I got this out.

I exhaled and started writing.

August 18, 2015—An Eight-Month Contract

I, Carrie Severson, promise to act upon preserving my fertility by May 1, 2016, if I am not in a relationship with a man I want to have children with. By taking action to preserve my fertility, I am giving me and my soul mate a better chance of creating a child together.

Carrie Severson

I taped the contract on the wall of my closet behind a few dresses. I wasn't going to forget about it, but I didn't want to see it every day. I didn't really want anyone else seeing it, either, in the event anyone was ever in my closet. It was by far the most important, vulnerable, life-changing piece of paper I owned.

Days went by, and I couldn't really get out of the funk I had found myself in. One night, I decided to turn to my writing group. I casually posted about the toxic night and conversation with Jay and ended with a little promise to myself that I was going to write about the weird date and the awkward but incredibly important follow-up conversation.

After I posted, I plugged my phone in and went to bed.

The next morning, when I checked in with my group, I was blown away by what I found. There were several hundred comments from women around the world who had been on similar dates. There were comments from women who'd had to defend their life and age to family and friends, men, and other women. And then there was a comment from an editor at a national magazine I wanted to write for.

Her comment was super simple:

> *Carrie, I just had a similar experience. I'd love to help you form this into an essay. Please contact me.*

I screamed and jumped up and down and called my mom. I had always wanted to break into the magazine market as a writer, and never in a million years had I thought going on a bad date would create that breakthrough.

I looked up the phone number of the magazine and dialed. I left a message with the editor's assistant and waited. Later that day, while sitting at a coffee shop, the editor called me back.

The first thing she said to me was, "Hi, Carrie! I know your work."

I couldn't believe it. We'd had such similar paths. We'd both chased down our dreams and career agendas. We were having a conversation about burnout before our love lives and the men we dated on the way to finding our forever partner. Then we agreed on a direction for my essay, and I spent the next week pouring out my heart on paper. The assignment gave me such clarity about my love life and about the dating patterns of single people.

There were so many women like me around the country. We ran after our careers the first chance we had. Millions of Generation X women were still single in their late thirties, and we were all now looking at our love lives.

I had never imagined that by chasing the void of my own career aspirations, I would find myself unable to manifest the one thing I wanted the most: a soul alliance I could call my home for the rest of my days.

I turned in my essay and waited for weeks for it to be published. I got word from my editor that the piece was ready to launch while standing in line to board a plane to visit a friend for a girls' weekend.

And as soon as I took my seat, I saw it. I let out a quick squeal and startled the woman sitting next to me. I apologized to her and explained that my first published essay for a women's magazine was online. She sat up, asked to read the piece, and ordered two cocktails to celebrate me. She even took a picture of me holding my tablet with the essay on the screen.

It was so sweet—two strangers celebrating a fun little win in life. It didn't feel like a win just for me, though. It felt like a win for authenticity, for love, for women my age.

The response from that essay was powerful, vast, and impactful. Hundreds of women reached out to me. I could classify their responses three different ways:

1. They used my piece as an invitation to tell me their own love and/or motherhood stories. I love that. I encourage that. I'm inspired by that. Stories connect us, and that response was what I'd hoped for.
2. They were angry with Jay.
3. They thought I was writing from a place of desperation and felt it necessary to encourage me to keep my head up and my heart open.

I always liked, loved, or responded with a thoughtful and kind remark. And then, out of the blue, I heard from a man. He had found my essay randomly one afternoon. He had been moving through a difficult breakup and felt compelled to read about my journey. His note to me was pretty simple:

Rest assured, not all men think that way. As a fortysome-thing man who has never been married and is without children, I get similar responses. Having spent the better

part of twenty years career driven, I am now taking a step
back and re-evaluating what has been important versus
what is important. Good luck with your search.

Something about that note struck me pretty deeply. I am a
searcher. I've always been one. I spent an entire year of soul quest-
ing to find my purpose in life. I've searched for friends and soul
mates. I've searched for business opportunities. And over the
years, I've come to believe that we're all searching. We're searching for soulful connections and alliances. We're searching for light
and love and little moments that give us a reason to celebrate our
humanity. We're searching for ways to contribute to the world, to
successfully leave our legacy and imprint.

Acknowledging the unknown and how connected everyone is
to it has brought some magical little pieces to my life. Expanding
my own awareness of how connected I am to everyone else has
allowed me to grow more comfortable in this unknown space.
Ever since recovering from burnout and fulfilling that first contract, I've found comfort in accepting myself as a searcher, and
in that moment, I knew on a cellular level that it was time to start
my next soul quest. But this time I'd put all my energy into my
love life and follow my internal GPS and whatever signs I saw
from God.

Chapter Ten

THAT DOCTOR

THAT STORY ABOUT MY REALLY BAD DATE OPENED THE DOOR to write for other national women's magazines. From there, I expanded my portfolio and wrote for many more. I took on assignments, had fun with my writing career, and even wrote about burnout from a healthy distance.

After a year, my attention was less on the nonprofit and more on helping other women share their stories. I wasn't expecting it or wanting to, but the demand was there. Women all over the United States e-mailed me for help getting their stories published. I took it as a sign from the Big U that I'd accomplished what I'd set out to do with Severson Sisters and that chapter of my life was at a close. It was safe to do something new.

I closed the nonprofit in 2016. Shortly after, I called a handful of leaders in the Phoenix area and invited them to my home. I asked them if they'd be willing to be a beta group for me as I worked out the details of what I could offer in a storytelling course.

For the next month, I held free storytelling classes in my home for eight women. Having been in the storytelling space for decades, I've developed a sixth sense for them. I imagine artists are that way with a blank canvas or musicians when they sit down to play something. There's electricity in the air when a story starts. I can feel it when it's going to be a good one, and I wanted to help others share their stories.

One afternoon, I received an e-mail from a woman I hadn't spoken to in ten years, maybe more. She'd heard I had started a storytelling business and wondered if I could help her wrap her mind around a few new story concepts. I agreed and sent her a few links to my published work, one of them being the piece about my date with Jay.

Within the hour, she sent me a string of text messages, all urging me to call her fertility doctor. Her doctor had helped her get pregnant twice, and she'd said if anyone could help me preserve my fertility, it was him. Then she sent me a link to the fertility specialist's website.

I let it sit on my screen for some time. I didn't respond to her, but I didn't look away, either. I couldn't think. I knew I had to do something. I was turning thirty-eight in a few months. It was now or never.

I went into my closet and pulled a few dresses out to see the contract I'd made with myself. I had to fulfill this one.

I wanted a child.

I wanted a family.

I wanted the possibility of raising a family with someone.

And I wanted the possibility of raising a child *I created* with someone.

Before I felt the anger, shame, embarrassment, and sadness weigh down on me that I was nowhere closer to what I craved than I had been a year earlier, I sat down at my computer and pulled up the doctor's website.

As luck would have it, the doctor was offering a free seminar in his office that weekend. If I wanted to come in to meet him and see what this whole preservation experience would be like, all I had to do was RSVP.

Before my brain convinced me otherwise, I drafted an e-mail to the address provided on the RSVP request and introduced myself. I asked if there was an opening in the seminar for me.

Within a matter of minutes, I received a reply. The office manager wanted to know more about me. Was I married? Was I going to be bringing someone with me?

Just me. Is there room? Thanks.

I received another reply, and this one urged me to bring a loved one. *For emotional support,* the message read.

My parents had purchased a second home not far from my place. They were officially considered "snowbirds" of Arizona. I loved it, and since my mom was in town, I RSVP'd for her. Because what single, nearly-thirty-eight-year-old doesn't bring her mom with her to learn about egg preservation?

As soon as I sent the e-mail, a mountain of tears broke free.

I cried because I didn't want to have to take action on this unknown new phase.

I cried because I didn't want to believe I had missed my chance as Jay had said.

I cried because I knew this was going to be the biggest investment I would have to make and I didn't have the money.

I cried because I was tired of dating. I cried because I hated that I felt so defeated.

Luckily, I didn't have to see anyone that day, so I gave in to the sadness and feeling of defeat. I shut off my computer, feelings, and mind, then climbed into bed and slept until the next day.

I couldn't shake the swell of tears the next morning, though, either. I'd burst into an ugly, sobbing mess with every other sigh.

After my second cup of coffee, I called my mom and asked if she had already gone for her walk. I had caught her just in time, and she was excited I wanted to go with her.

I brushed my teeth, did what I could to wash the evidence of my tears away, and threw on yoga pants. I couldn't form a thought on the drive to my parents'. My brain was blank.

My mom was waiting for me in her driveway when I pulled up, which was handy since that meant I didn't have to take my sunglasses off and show her my puffy, bloodshot eyes.

I don't remember the walk. I don't remember what was said before we turned around to head back to her house. I knew I had to bring up the fertility clinic, though.

"An old friend of mine read my essay about Jay yesterday."

"The one you wrote last year?"

"Yep."

"Wow! What'd she think?"

"She sent me the contact information for her fertility specialist."

My mom didn't say anything.

"I checked out the site, and they have a free seminar about egg preservation on Saturday," I went on. "I RSVP'd for it. Will you come with me?"

"Yes, I think that's a good decision."

"I think it's time to learn more about it."

The rest of the walk could have been incredibly eventful, but I don't remember anything else. My brain was blank again. I couldn't concentrate on a thing until that Saturday.

I woke up before the sun and was on my third cup of coffee by the time I was ready to jump in the shower and get ready for the seminar. I wore an orange dress and my favorite sandals.

My mom came to get me, and I navigated us there with plenty of time to spare. The office was tucked away in the corner of a medical complex, and there were three couples sitting in the waiting room when we walked in. The silence in the lobby was heavy with such heartache. It felt like a funeral.

I wrote my name down on a *Hello, my name is . . .* sticker and sat at the end of a bench with my mom. We were the last to arrive and thankfully didn't have to wait long before being brought back to the seminar area.

There were eight folding chairs set up.

My mom and I got the first row. I took the chair closest to the wall.

We sat there waiting for a handful of minutes, but it felt like hours. Nobody said a word. It was uncomfortable to even let out a slight sigh or shift in my chair, as I was afraid the sound would echo throughout the room.

The office manager came out and excused the doctor for running behind a few minutes. She said he was in the kitchen making his tea.

And then the office manager walked over to me and extended her hand. "Hi, Carrie. We communicated over e-mail earlier this week."

"Hello, hi! Yes, I remember."

"I just have to tell you how brave this is of you. I wish more single women did this."

I nodded and smiled.

She walked away.

The heaviness among us eight thickened a few layers after that. I looked over my shoulder at the other women, and they were all fidgeting. Nobody met my eyes.

I searched for them. I wanted to feel more community in that room. I wasn't the only brave one. I felt segregated from the rest, though, because of my single status, and that made me feel all sorts of things I didn't want to in that moment.

My heart beat faster.

My jaw clenched, and my fingernails pressed against the palms of my hands.

Brave.

Am I brave?

Is this even an act of bravery?

It didn't feel brave. I felt betrayed. I was angry I hadn't met the man I was going to make babies with and that I was here out of desperation, out of fear of Jay being right. I wasn't being brave. I was afraid. It felt more like a Hail Mary. It was my safety net.

After all, the office manager did what every other person I'd ever met did: she put me—and every other single, thirtysomething woman—in a different category than married women.

When his tea was ready, the doctor came out and gave us a lecture on how cells, veins, sperm, eggs, and age all played a role in baby making. When he was finished, he asked if anyone had any questions.

One woman asked what the doctor would do if she wasn't able to carry a baby to term. Another woman asked what he would do if she wasn't able to conceive. I asked about preservation.

He invited each of us to his office for a quick private consult to get more specifics about our cases. Before I made my way back, Ms. Office Manager came back for round two.

"What did you think of his presentation?" she asked.

"Very informative," my mom said.

"Interesting," I said.

"You know, at your age, you should really consider freezing embryos, too, as a frozen egg only has a 30 percent chance of making it to a live birth." And she walked away again.

I looked at my mom. "What did she just say?"

"I think she just suggested you buy sperm."

And before that idea could sink in past shock, it was my turn to talk to the doctor.

My talk with the doctor was a review of what the last ninety minutes had been about. And he agreed with his office manager's suggestion to create embryos.

Sperm.

Again.

Always with the sperm.

I couldn't remember the last time I said the word *sperm*, let alone as often as I did in one conversation.

"Where do the embryos and eggs get stored?" I asked.

The doctor explained that I had to pay for a storage container per year at a facility. The eggs and embryos could be stored for fifteen years.

I looked at him. "What happens after fifteen years?"

"We dispose of them for you with your permission."

Dispose of them.

My breath caught. The doctor said it without any explanation or hesitation. I could feel a floodgate of emotion about to burst just under the surface of my rib cage. It was stuck in my cells and aching in my heart. My skin crawled.

I clenched my fists and pulsed my fingernails in my palms to keep the tears safely tucked away.

I was shocked. I was confused. He would dispose of a little piece of my soul if I didn't implant the embryo in fifteen years. And I had to keep paying for a storage facility until I decided what to do. But with my permission, he'd get rid of it.

I was at capacity, and the doctor clearly knew it. I couldn't absorb or hear anything else.

Before I left the doctor's office, I was told of the $5,000 summer special they were having and was reminded that if I decided to create and freeze embryos, the price would be higher.

It was like the first day of every school year, date, and job all rolled into a two-hour experience. I didn't ask for more information about their summer special. It all started to feel like a big semi-annual sale at a department store.

Act Now.

Save Now.

Buy this and you'll save 10 percent . . .

I thanked everyone for their time and energy and said I'd be in touch. Before I left, I received a printed sheet of paper that read:

Subject:

A thirty-seven-year-old female. She has been regular with five days of moderate flow. She presents to consider freezing eggs and making embryos. She is not in a relationship. She had AMH tested, and this was over seven. She is aware of her AMA status and the impact on chromosomally abnormal embryos, and we discussed the near 60 percent likelihood of aneuploidy in her blasts at her age. Egg freezing would lessen the percent of viable embryos in total. She has been in good health overall, except in 2013, she had fatigue and was noted to have low T3.

There it all was. Even my relationship status made its way onto the summary of my uterus.

My mom and I drove to a new restaurant we wanted to try out. We ordered and sat in silence for a while. I could have sat in silence longer, but my mom broke the seal and we couldn't go back.

"I think the sperm is a good idea," my mom said.

"Why is that?"

"What if your husband has issues and he's the reason you can't have children of your own? This way you'd have a child that is at least part of your union."

It made sense to me.

Preservation was my plan B. And now I could create a plan C. With my mom in my corner, I felt like I could breathe again.

I leaned back and exhaled as big as I could. I could still see myself as a sixteen-year-old girl standing in my childhood bedroom. She wanted to do something really big with her life. She knew she was meant for grand things—light, lots of feelings, and big connections. She never imagined she'd be sitting at lunch years later talking to her mom about a sperm donor.

But there we were, planning to preserve my fertility and buy sperm to create embryos.

It was by far the weirdest day of my life.

I bet it was one of the weirdest days of my mom's life, too.

I ate my lunch. I felt everything. I scanned my body and could taste the flavor of disappointment, shame, fear, excitement, and a slight hint of empowerment.

Chapter Eleven

THE EMBRYOS

GAVE MYSELF THE REST OF THAT SATURDAY AND SUNDAY to process what I had learned at the fertility office, and on Monday morning, I e-mailed the fertility clinic with a dozen or so questions.

Was there an embryo donation agency somewhere I could donate embryos to?

Where do I buy sperm?

Now what?

The ironic thing about preserving my fertility was that I didn't have time to really process the act of preservation in itself. I was making life-changing decisions by the minute. Despite the fact that I had spent the previous year preparing to preserve my fertility, a part of me was still holding on to hope I wouldn't have to. I still couldn't believe I was there.

Time sat on my chest, and it became heavier with each day. I could feel the pressure of it all. It was thick and made it hard to inhale deeply. All I could do was educate myself about the process and pray I was doing the right thing for myself, my future self, and this man, if he ever came along, not to mention the embryos that would one day be leading their own lives.

The embryos.

My soul and someone else's soul would meet in a petri dish in the back room of a fertility clinic. It wasn't how I saw myself creating another soul, but it was where my journey was taking me. I wanted to be informed about every step of the process before starting this new chapter.

Later that day, the office manager of the fertility clinic e-mailed me back and gave me details about their available dates and how often I would need to come in for an ultrasound. She didn't know anything about an embryo donation agency but did provide me with the name and number for a sperm bank.

So that was my next phone call.

I introduced myself and explained my situation. After sharing the news that I was considering embryo preservation, I was congratulated. And then I was given a username and password and walked through their online database of men who had donated sperm.

Sadly, the sperm bank didn't know of an embryo donation agency offhand, either.

I browsed through pages and pages and pages of sperm donors. Each profile picture was from their childhood, which I was actually grateful for. I didn't want to know what they looked like as grown men. It was already starting to feel like a really twisted dating app.

Women Who Want a Baby meets Baby Daddy.

I couldn't get myself to click the "More Information" button on any of the donor profiles. I didn't want to do that alone.

I kept digging for answers to my embryo donation questions, and after many days found an agency that had started in 1997. I found as much out about the process as I could and then sent them an e-mail.

> *Hello,*
>
> *My name is Carrie Severson. I'm single, nearly thirty-eight, and have decided to preserve my fertility. I'm having my eggs retrieved and frozen, and I'm moving forward with fertilizing eggs. I'd like to ensure I have a plan for the embryos if I do not end up using them. If I were to move forward with your agency, can you tell me what to anticipate?*
>
> *Carrie Severson*

I hit "send" and put my computer down, trying to find the feeling of empowerment in all of this. I was making decisions I'd never imagined I would have to make, and I wanted to feel better about it all. I wanted to feel the way I imagined a solid and strong feminist would feel. I could not get around the sense of loneliness, though. And the more information I learned, the heavier it weighed on me and the harder it crushed my spirit.

Meditation was one of the nonnegotiables that I turned to whenever I felt overwhelm set in so I crawled up into my oversized chair and crossed my legs. I took a deep breath and imagined God sitting in front of me.

"Tell me what to do," I said aloud.

I didn't hear anything back.

"Am I doing the right thing?"

I didn't hear anything back.

I squirmed in my seat. I didn't feel connected. I took another breath and imagined light floating through my body into my womb.

I tried talking to God again. "Show me how it is so that I easily know what right move to make next."

There was some pressure on my heart, and I took it as my answer. *Do what you can to follow your heart in this, and it'll all turn out okay.*

That was the best I could do. There wasn't a road map for this new soul quest of mine. My heart always longed for a family. It was what I always saw for myself. I wanted a family with my best friend and soul mate, and my heart had led me to this place in life.

Over the next two days, I spent a lot of time in my meditation chair. I turned a cookie sheet upside down, put my tablet on top of it, and balanced it on my legs while sitting crisscrossed. I was grateful for the safe space of my big chair when I saw the e-mail from the embryo donation agency pop up.

Hello, Carrie,

Thank you for your interest in our program. We do have an option for families to place their remaining embryos in the event that their plans change. It sounds like this might be the option you are looking for. If so, we would need you to wait to complete the necessary forms with us until after all the embryos are created (the eggs are fertilized and frozen in storage). Once this occurs, you can follow the instructions attached, and we can make sure that your embryos find a good home. Please feel welcome to contact me with any further questions or concerns.

Then I was sent a list of things to remember to do if this was the course of action I was going to take. The list included the following:

- Complete any forms that my doctor needs
- Send any and all medical forms to the donation agency
- Make an appointment to have the FDA's required infectious disease testing for donors
- Complete a Donor Risk Factor Questionnaire
- Create a will that includes the embryos

A will? I had to create a will that would advocate for the embryos in the event that I died before the embryos were implanted or adopted. I let that soak in, and I embraced the depth of that decision. It rocked me. It scared me. And all the what-ifs finally showed up.

What if the embryos were adopted by a couple who mistreated them growing up? What if the embryo wanted to meet the dad? What if I had a mental breakdown years from now and regretted all of this? What if the embryos grew up to resent me for doing this?

The questions I couldn't possibly answer just swirled round and round in my mind.

I took some deep inhales and held each one for three seconds. When I exhaled, I imagined the anxiety, the fog, the heartache, the stress, and the pressure I had absorbed over the last few weeks dislodging from my cells and disappearing into the atmosphere. I imagined myself surrounded by a pink bubble filled with sparkles and butterflies. I saw myself a decade older. I was happy. I was married. I had children. We were a beautiful family unit. We were outside sitting at a picnic table laughing. I felt safe and deeply loved.

I thought of the embryos. I imagined them each as a living, breathing human. Some were boys, others girls. They were all happy, and they were all safe and deeply loved.

I could feel those kids. I could see them as if they were standing in front of me. I could hear them laughing. And I hadn't even created them yet. I felt at peace with the idea of never meeting them. If I ended up meeting someone and creating a family some other way, I was at peace moving forward with this whole thing.

Sobs poured out of me from a place so deep I hadn't felt it before. Sobs I had been holding back for years had found a way to break free, at last. I let my anger and resentment come to the surface. My jaw tightened, and the muscles in my back, arms, and fingers tensed.

I imagined my pink bubble of sparkles and butterflies soaking into my skin and blending into my blood. The sparkles ignited my cells and massaged my bones, organs, and muscles and surrounded my heart in a big, warm embrace. The warmth made my legs and arms tingle. I felt a buzzing around my cheeks and chest.

The anger and resentment were less present now, and I could see how safe I was in this new chapter of my life.

I couldn't understand why my journey was the way it was, but I could lean into this new chapter with a different viewpoint.

And finally, I had found the empowerment bubble I'd been craving.

With a clearer sense of my emotions, I was able to make a plan for myself. Plan C involved so much more than plan B and required so much more of me.

As the office manager had told me, frozen eggs have a 30 percent chance of making it to a live birth, but embryos have a better chance of meeting the world. And this whole journey had started because I wanted to create more time for myself and my future self so I would have the option to raise a biological family.

Each decision I made in this process was inundated with major turning points.

My 2016 Fertility List

- *Tell Dad.*
- *Tell siblings.*
- *Tell my friends.*
- *Find sperm donor.*
- *Get FDA blood work done.*
- *Retrieve eggs.*
- *Write a story about this.*
- *Fall in love.*

After I got the blessing from my family, I called my friends and asked them to support me as I went through this new chapter of my soul quest. I invited a handful of them to my home on a Saturday to help me select a sperm donor.

On the day of my little celebration, four of my girlfriends came to cheer me on. We went through a handful of donors. My friends didn't weigh in on who they felt would be best, but rather, they asked me question after question about my feelings and dreams. They were more interested in my mental state than anything else.

After several hours of girl talk, I made my decision. I selected a donor.

When my friends left, I sent an e-mail to the fertility clinic and told them I was ready to move forward as I'd found a donor. On Monday, I received a response that listed times I could come in to sign the paperwork and check to see if my body was ready to start the journey.

I read the e-mail over and over again, searching for the support and human emotion. It sounded so cold. As an empath, I craved more connection to the process and to the people I was in this process with. It was entirely too medical and scientific. Everyone I dealt with lacked heart and warmth and basic human social skills. I wasn't making easy, everyday decisions, but it was a business for the fertility doctors, managers, and technicians. They piled women into their office for appointments just like mine. I wasn't assigned a case manager or even introduced to the women in the office.

I responded to take the first date possible and booked it in my calendar. I did everything I could for the next few days to keep my mind occupied, but really, my CEO-wired brain started critiquing how they managed their business. And I wasn't impressed. That should have told me something about what I was about to do, but for better or worse, these people were on my soul quest for a reason.

I went to the appointment by myself. First, they did an ultrasound. The scan showed I had a cyst in one of my ovaries, which meant I couldn't start the fertility cycle yet. We had to wait until it was gone, something that should happen on its own when I started my next period.

Next was the very overwhelming paperwork. A new technician went over the contract with me, turning this very medical, scientific process into a legal one. The technician had been hired the week before and breezed through the contract in a way that kept us friends and in an informal setting. I never heard her talk about the price of fertility drugs or say that I would have to go to a special pharmacy to get drugs. She treated me like a girlfriend, like I was about to sign a note in class to pass on to the cute guy sitting next to us. She wasn't qualified in any way to take me through a contract, but I hadn't thought of bringing a lawyer with me. In hindsight, I should have asked to take the contract home, but I hadn't thought of that, either.

I signed the contract and went home to wait for my period to come so I could start injecting myself with the fertility drugs. It was pretty anticlimactic, really.

That was, until I received a phone call later that day from a representative at a pharmacy I had never heard of. She told me her office had just received an order for me that totaled $6,000 and wanted to confirm it before she started filling it.

I had agreed to preserve my fertility for $5,000 and assumed the drugs were included in that. At no point did anyone tell me there would be an additional cost of $6,000 to pay for the fertility shots I would have to take.

I told the pharmacy representative that she was mistaken, and I thanked her for her time.

As soon as I hung up, I called the fertility clinic and asked to talk to the office manager. She came on after several minutes of me waiting on hold. I explained there was no way I'd pay for drugs costing an additional $6,000. I explained that nobody at her office had told me about this cost and I wasn't going to pay for it.

She said that she would knock $1,000 off their retrieval price to make the overall investment easier for me to reach, but insisted I find a way to pay for the fertility drugs. The procedure wouldn't work any other way. She repeated over and over again that the drugs were the only way I'd be able to preserve my fertility.

And after several minutes of listening to her, my empowerment bubble started fading and I gave in.

I believed her.

I called my mom and told her about this disappointing turn of events. We agreed that this was still a smart move for me as I turned thirty-eight, and my parents offered to lend me half the money for the fertility drugs.

I hung up the phone and collapsed on my bed. I knew all too well what I was about to do. I was chasing money, and that felt similar to what I'd lived through for the sake of the nonprofit. The money was always just on the other side of it all. Sometimes I was aligned with it. Sometimes it was easy to find. But right there, right then, I couldn't think of a reputable way to make $3,000 in ten days.

I couldn't shake the feeling of disappointment.

The anger I had felt about my own journey was back. If I hadn't launched the nonprofit, I would have the money to do this. But there I was in a ball on my bed. And guilt grabbed hold of me for not having *enough*.

The end goal was still the same. I wanted the opportunity to have a family, but while the men in my life were fun, they were men to have flings with, not serious relationships. There wasn't one man in the picture who I could see having a future or babies with. Egg preservation and embryo creation was a smart move.

Still, the guilt won that day, and I pulled a blanket over my head and let myself fall asleep.

When I woke up the next morning, I was in the same position. I hadn't moved at all during the night. I scanned my body, searching for the darkness and the guilt. I felt it in my heart and around my belly. I couldn't take a deep breath in or out, and I didn't try to force it.

I splashed some water on my face and avoided my eyes in the mirror. I made myself a coffee and grabbed my computer. I pulled up the instructions the fertility clinic had given me and called the pharmacy. I asked the representative for the exact cost of each drug and how long each one would last me. Since I had to go into the fertility office every three days for an ultrasound to check my progress, I figured I could break the cost of the drugs up into three or four sections to give myself some time to come up with $3,000.

The first round of drugs would cost me $1,900. I agreed to pick them up in a few days.

Next, I made a list of every client I had. I made notes next to the ten clients I knew could use my help. I let myself daydream and think of a way that I could earn $3,000 so I could make this investment while also serving these ten people. I created a special package for them that included a sixty-minute call and ghostwriting a personal essay. I also offered to pitch the personal essay to outlets through my contacts to increase its chances of being published.

I priced it at $300 per package and sent personal notes out to each of the clients. Five of the ten ladies responded to me within the day with a solid and grateful YES! I booked them all in my calendar within the next few days to ensure my hormones wouldn't be a problem as I worked with them. As each payment came through, I felt lighter and lighter. And by the time I went to pick up my fertility shots at the end of the week and officially start my treatment cycle, I had made another few hundred dollars. I had to put the rest on my credit cards and pray cash came in fast.

The feeling of being so dependent on money was such a familiar one, and the further I got into the process, the heavier I felt both physically and emotionally. I had to constantly remind myself why I was putting myself back into this ring of fire.

I wanted the possibility of babies.

I wanted the possibility of a family.

Since my forever home and husband weren't anywhere to be seen, I was putting myself through this mess to buy us time.

The drugs went into the fridge, and every time I gave myself a shot, I would think of what my life could look like with a family. I rolled the vial between my fingers. I'd talk out loud to myself in a loving manner. I'd take my time as I cleaned my skin, and before I pinched myself, I'd take a big inhale and longer exhale.

Injection.

Within days of starting the hormones, my body felt broken. I felt broken. It's common for women who go through fertility treatment to have a bad reaction to the drugs, and I was one of those women.

My immune system hadn't been strong to begin with due to the burnout, and I was going through this whole experience by myself. I had to talk to the doctor by myself. I sat in the lobby by myself while watching other women be comforted by their people. The added stress of the treatment and cost of the drugs just tipped me over the edge. My body was hurt and angry.

Within ten days of being on fertility drugs, I had put on a dress size and a bra size, and hated everyone who came within twenty feet of me. The closer I got to the end of the cycle, the worse I felt, too. The excess hormones flowing through my veins made everything harder.

My last scheduled doctor's appointment prior to my egg retrieval finally came. I had been on fertility drugs for eleven days and anticipated good news from the cold and uncompassionate technician who stuck a wand up my lady parts every other day. As I drove to the fertility clinic, I imagined how it'd feel hearing about a whole butt-load of good-sized eggs just waiting to be harvested.

Instead, the technician said I had eight eggs, and the doctor thought it was best for me to stay on the drugs for at least another two days.

Rage.

Hostility.

Get your wand out of my lady parts, you dirty little bitch.

I added up the cost of another two days of drugs—$1,000. It was all I had left in the bank and on a credit card. I sobbed and screamed and demanded to see the doctor.

He met me in the conference room and told me that if I didn't do another two days, this whole thing would be for nothing. He wanted the best for me, and if we went into the retrieval as planned, I might get a few embryos at most. Sitting there, trying to listen to him without rage pulsing through my cells, I agreed.

The pharmacy was waiting for me when I showed up to grab two more days' worth of fertility drugs. I split the cost between two cards and called my mom. She reminded me to keep calm and that we'd deal with the cost later.

Day twelve. I shot myself up morning, noon, and night. And that afternoon, something new happened. I broke out in hives. My arms and legs were covered in bumps, my skin was hot, and I felt a little fatigued. I sent an e-mail to the fertility team and waited for a response. Still nothing by the time the office closed. I called the emergency number I was given and left a message explaining that the shots had given me hives and that they were worsening as the day went on.

I got a call back from the technician within the hour. She told me she was out at a bar and would call the doctor to ask what I should do. She hung up, and I waited at my kitchen table for next steps.

A few minutes later, my phone rang again. I could barely hear the technician on the other end, but I managed to make out her words as she said, "You probably ovulated early so the doctor wants you to come in first thing in the morning for the procedure. I'll meet you at the clinic at 7:00 a.m."

The technician reminded me that I couldn't drive myself home after the procedure as I'd be under heavy sedation.

I hung up the phone and called my mom. She was out of town and couldn't get a flight back that night. We talked about as much as we could, and she talked me down off the ledge I was standing on. I felt as if I were walking on shards of glass and everything I did was wrong. And here I was, about to lose everything because my body went into early ovulation.

The fact that I didn't have anyone to take me to this procedure was a reminder of how alone I had felt throughout this entire experience. With the pulsing river of hormones running through my veins, I couldn't hold back the mountain of tears and screams just beneath the surface.

I let it out.

All of it.

I changed my clothes and fell into bed that night. I got a few hours of sleep before I had to get in the car and get to the clinic.

On the ride there, I prayed to everyone I could think of.

Please let this go okay.

Please help me through this.

And when I pulled into the parking lot, I sent a text to my friend Eileen and told her I needed a ride home. She responded immediately with a thumbs-up and agreed to bring me home.

The doctor was waiting for me with a team of nurses when I arrived at the clinic. I got changed, and he explained that he was going to go in and retrieve what he could. His hope was that he wasn't too late. His hope was that he caught the early ovulation in time and I still had eggs ready and ripe.

We talked about the best-case scenario and agreed on a percentage of eggs he would turn into embryos. I said to keep 40 percent as eggs and turn 60 percent into embryos.

The last thing I remember was counting backward as a cold, prickly rush ran down my right arm into my hand.

When I woke up, I was surrounded by nurses. The doctor was in the room, too. Before I was fully awake, I asked him what had happened.

It was the worst-case scenario. I had ovulated early.

I had lost everything but three underdeveloped eggs.

He retrieved the three underdeveloped eggs and was doing what he could to help them develop a little further in petri dishes. Even in my haze, I was heartbroken, angry, disappointed, and full of blame.

The nurses helped me get dressed and called my friend into the back room to get me. I can't remember how I got from the procedure room into the car. I vaguely remember telling Eileen that the doctor had failed. I remember saying this whole thing had been for nothing. I remember expressing my disappointment.

The next memory I have is of being on the couch in my living room. I was in pain, holding my belly and moaning. Eileen was in the kitchen getting me water, and her daughter stood in front of me, watching me, telling Eileen every move I made. I pushed myself up and was able to stand for a minute before collapsing backward into the cushions.

I told Eileen I had to vomit. She helped me stand up and walked with me into the bathroom. Her daughter stood outside the door, and Eileen held my hair back while I made my way to the floor. When vomit came out my nose and up my throat, I felt a warmth rushing into my underwear. I was bleeding. I had been told that I may have some spotting and to prepare for it with panty liners or pads, so I told Eileen I thought I was bleeding and she got a pad ready for me. I flushed the toilet, and she helped me turn around. I pulled my pants down and blood came flowing out of me into the toilet. I could hear it hitting the water. I looked up at her and saw the pain in her face, which I guessed was a reflection of mine.

This was more than bleeding; this was hemorrhaging.

She immediately grabbed her phone and called the doctor. Eileen left. I sat there bleeding into the toilet and vomiting into the garbage can. She came back into the bathroom to check on me. I leaned back on the toilet and apologized for throwing up in the garbage can. She took it and washed it out in the kitchen sink, then rushed back into the bathroom to tell me about her conversation with the fertility clinic.

After noting how unprofessional and uncompassionate the woman she spoke to was, Eileen said all the fertility team could do was have the doctor call me back. She also called my mom and sister to tell them what was happening. My mom was in Wisconsin, and my sister, like most of my friends, was at work. She lived with her husband in Phoenix but wasn't available just yet. It was clear we needed help, though, and someone had to show up fast.

We sat in the bathroom waiting, listening to the blood hit the toilet water. Eileen answered her phone after the first ring, and I could hear the urgency in her voice. She put the phone on speaker, and I recognized the doctor's voice.

He asked me if it felt like the worst period I'd ever had or if I had a sense there was something more happening. I'd had cramps with periods since I was eleven years old but never anything this severe. He said there's always a slight chance the bleeding women experience afterward will be alarming, but it should subside within a few days. In the meantime, all I could do was use pads and be gentle on my body. Move slow. Don't exercise. Rest a lot. He called in a prescription for morphine that I could use for the pain, but there wasn't anything he could do for the bleeding now.

Eileen thanked the doctor and hung up. I didn't have the energy or grace to give him. I was half-naked, which wasn't anything new to him, but I felt more exposed and rawer in that moment than ever before.

Eileen left the bathroom again and called my mom to update her.

I didn't say much to my mom. I knew she felt bad for not being there with me in such a big moment of my life. She did what she could from Wisconsin, though. She hung up the phone to call her handyman here in Phoenix, hoping he'd do her a favor. Our circle of crisis was getting bigger and bigger, and had officially crossed state lines. My mom's handyman agreed to go to the drugstore to pick up the drugs for me. If I hadn't been in so much pain, bleeding, puking, and in a drug-infused haze, I would have been either humiliated or grateful.

Neither Eileen nor I anticipated my postprocedure recovery would go the way it did. We were told to anticipate me getting lots of sleep, watching lots of TV, and needing lots of comfort food. We weren't expecting to have to make a run to the drugstore for heavy-duty painkillers or to need someone to stay with me all day because painkillers can easily make everything go downhill fast. Plus, Eileen is a mother of six children and had to leave at a certain point to pick her kids up from school.

After the handyman showed up with the drugs, Eileen called my sister. Someone had to come for the second shift of Carrie's Uterus Crisis.

After some time, the nausea eased and I could leave the bathroom. The bleeding continued for hours, though. Eileen laid towels down on the couch so if I bled through, I wouldn't stain the cushions. She covered me with a few blankets and gave me some oatmeal to eat before my first dose of morphine.

My sister took off work a few hours early and arrived in time for Eileen to go get her children from school. I thanked her and her daughter for helping me so much and told her I'd call her when I could process everything.

Holly came and snuggled on the couch with me. I told her as much as I could remember and leaned into her when the sobbing started. I couldn't get past the part where I had to tell her about the underdeveloped eggs and the experience being such a failure.

She held me and let me cry, and at some point, I drifted off to sleep.

When I woke up, my brother-in-law was there with food and my car keys. He picked up my car from the clinic and brought me spaghetti and meatballs, garlic bread, chicken noodle soup, and lots of crackers. I could hear him unpacking the groceries in my kitchen. He plated me a huge helping of spaghetti, meatballs, and garlic bread. We all watched an episode of *Bones* and when the sun started to set, they gave me another painkiller, tucked me into bed, made sure my phone was right next to me, and took off.

I didn't wake up until the next morning, still bleeding and heartbroken.

I made it through half the morning before surrendering to a painkiller. I promised myself I would only take them when the physical pain outweighed the emotional one, and that morning, pain was there with every deep breath I took.

Chapter Twelve

THE SECOND ROUND

FOR THE NEXT FEW DAYS, MY LIFE CONSISTED OF SOAKED MEN-strual pads, reruns of *Chuck*, junk food, and tidal waves of emotions ranging from depression to sadness to guilt to anger.

I made sure I showered every day.

I made sure I ate every day.

I made sure I answered the phone when anyone who knew what had happened called me.

Beyond that, I lived moment to moment.

After my shower each morning, I examined my body in the mirror. I'd run my hands over my belly and cradle it. I'd think of the three underdeveloped eggs in a petri dish whenever I touched my belly. My body resembled one that had just given birth. My womb had done some work. Someone had taken something out of her, and she was sassy, sore, and swollen.

I didn't wear anything but yoga pants and oversized T-shirts for the next week. It was the only outfit I felt comfortable wearing. Plus, nothing else fit.

Before the procedure, I had stocked my fridge and cupboards with a combination of comfort food and healthy food. If my body had wanted it, I'd bought it. I ate single servings of oatmeal and soup. I snacked on gluten-free crackers and frozen treats that came on sticks.

As a self-development junkie, I knew my spirit had been crushed. I had work to do. The procedure had hurt me at my soul level. I could feel it deep within my bones. It wasn't cramps or the soreness that comes with bleeding; it was a puncture wound that extended through all parts of me. And I didn't have the energy to start another soul quest to heal the wound I was left with.

Despite the fact that my voice was stifled and I didn't have the heart or guts to let it out, I was truthful whenever someone called to check on me. I was blunt and said I was bleeding, sad, heartbroken, and tired, and that wasn't going to change overnight. I wished it would. I wanted nothing more than to hit fast-forward on my life and be healed, happy, and healthy again.

On day three postprocedure, I experienced a slight shift. My journal sat on the coffee table next to my couch. It had been there all along, but I had ignored it until that morning. I felt the urge to crack it open and capture a few things running through my soul. Before I had time to analyze anything, I grabbed a pen and wrote *How am I feeling now?* at the top of a page.

I stared at the blank page for a few beats, then let the words come to me.

Betrayed came in first. My gut twitched. I inhaled and held it for a second. When I exhaled, I thought of the word *robbed*.

And then . . .

> *Disgusted.*
> *Livid.*
> *Defeated.*
> *Helpless.*
> *Guilty.*
> *Ashamed.*
> *Embarrassed.*
> *Heavy.*
> *Disconnected.*
> *Vulnerable.*
> *Raw.*

Words kept coming to me.

> *Mother.*
> *Lost.*
> *Empty.*
> *Failure.*
> *Childless.*
> *Hurt.*

When I heard the word *supported* come to mind, I felt a little lighter. My heart ached but not because I was alone. My heart ached because I had dared to do something supportive of and aligned with my deepest dreams. Those dreams were still there. I couldn't change what had happened, and I didn't want to let go of my dreams of being a mom.

On the next page I wrote, *Do I blame the doctor?*

Blame hung on me like smog, and little strings of that blame were tied to him and his staff.

YES, I wrote. I blamed him. I didn't believe he'd caused me to ovulate early, but his team was green and uneducated. Someone should have known I was ready to go into retrieval before that day. I didn't believe I'd needed the extra two days of drugs. The doctor was greedy, and it felt like he was playing God. I did blame him that I only had underdeveloped eggs available to work with.

The darkness and grief I felt was heavy.

I examined my list of words. There were many that stood out to me that I wanted to lean into. I didn't have the bandwidth, though, in that moment. I put a star next to the words *guilty, vulnerable, failure,* and *lost*. I couldn't feel those words but trusted that they came to mind for a reason. They were underneath everything I could feel, and when the time was right, I'd come back to those four words and dig them up. First, though, I gave myself permission to sit and finish bleeding.

Over the next two days, the bleeding lightened up. Little by little, my belly deflated. By the time day five came, I felt like going to a Pilates class.

Day five post procedure was another big day. The doctor had said he'd call by the end of the fifth day to tell me the results of the eggs developing in the petri dishes. A small piece of my heart wished he wouldn't call. Whenever I thought of him, my skin crawled, my shoulder blades squeezed together, and my tongue pressed itself up against the roof of my mouth. Masking the betrayal, anger, and blame I felt for him wasn't going to be easy. I was trapped. I had to talk to him, and yet the last thing I ever wanted to do again was hear his voice.

As I pulled into the Pilates studio parking lot, my phone rang. I recognized the number as the fertility clinic. I parked the car, said a prayer, and answered. It was the scientist who had done the actual fertilization of the egg and sperm in the back room. I had met him once before. He reminded me of his name and told me he had the results. He was sorry to tell me that only one of the eggs had made it to the final stage.

My heart exploded with excitement. I had one! I had one trouper. This whole mess hadn't been for nothing. I screamed and shrieked. My joy was everywhere, and I was grateful for this update. He apologized again for the disappointing news. I didn't bother trying to convince him this was good, considering how devastated I'd been all week. We agreed that I would come in the next day to talk to the doctor and go over next steps and the pro- cedure in general.

Before I ran into the Pilates class, I called my mom to tell her the news. We laughed and exhaled together. I grabbed a reformer in the corner of the Pilates studio and informed the instructor about my recent womb experience. I was given the green light to do what felt good and take it easy.

Pilates was a combination of daydreaming and jungle-gym class. I avoided anything that would put pressure on my abs.

Instead, I stretched, laughed, and bounced. The rest of the class was doing One Hundreds, and I was in first position up against the bodyboard doing deep pliés. It was glorious and free. I could feel parts of my heart searching for the light again. The cracks were still there, but so was the light.

An hour passed, and then it was time to go back to real life.

The Pilates studio was sandwiched between a juice bar and a salad shop that made awesome salads. Since I hadn't eaten anything green in five full days, I grabbed as many of my favorite juices as I could and ordered a Greek salad for dinner. I loaded everything in the car and cranked up the music. With the windows down and a car full of food that would help me turn a corner, I headed home to prepare for a meeting with the doctor the next morning.

On the way back to my house, I focused on my breath to see if I could find the betrayal, loss, or anger for the whole ordeal. It was still there, but it felt further away. It felt more like a battle scar than something I had to process and give to God to deal with.

That night, I massaged my belly in the shower. I thanked it for going through this for us. I popped open a green juice and my salad, and plopped myself on the couch.

The meeting with the fertility team was at eight o'clock the next morning so I went to bed early and melted right into the mattress. I slept like a goddess that night.

The next morning I was welcomed back to his office by a technician I had never seen before. She told me she had just started and asked me if I needed a water or breakfast bar. I declined and made my way back to the office.

The doctor reached out to shake my hand and asked me how I was doing. We launched right into a conversation about how disappointed he was in the results of my procedure.

I leaned into his desk as much as possible. I could tell he was empathetic about my journey, and it took me by surprise to be met with depth and warmth. It was what I had wanted all along from his team. We were making babies. There isn't a more important decision in life, and I was doing it with people who didn't care about me.

But sitting across from him in my follow-up meeting, I could tell he also felt sorry for me. He called in his office manager, whom I never wanted to see again.

He turned his computer screen toward me to show me my chart. He shared a bunch of really scientific information with me about blood cells and vessels and the drug cocktail I had been on. He said that it was unfortunate that I'd ovulated early and eventually said, "We call what happened to you an escaped case. Your eggs simply escaped too early. I haven't had an escaped case in several years."

Tears started to pool in my tear ducts. I blinked them away. I cleared my throat, pulled my shoulder blades back, and shifted in my chair so I could push my tailbone harder against the metal.

Next, he pulled out a sheet of paper that showed the growth of my single embryo. Because he'd retrieved it as an underdeveloped egg, and due to the stress it had been put under, it was considered a Grade-C embryo.

"What does that mean?" I asked before he could get another word out.

Our faces were only a few feet apart. His eyes locked with mine. "It means it has a really high probability of having abnormalities and a much lower chance of resulting in a live birth. We don't recommend you ever use this embryo."

I leaned back in my chair and pursed my lips. My toes curled under. My butt tightened. I held my breath. The bubble I had stepped into the night before popped. I uncrossed my legs and pushed my tailbone into the metal chair again.

Discomfort. Anything to keep from crying in front of these two people.

My thoughts were getting the best of me in that moment, and then I heard him tell me he wanted to offer me the chance to do it again. And for this round, he'd donate his time. I still had to pay for the drugs, but I'd get a second retrieval and embryo attempt out of the deal if I wanted.

We stared at each other. I searched for an answer. And finally, I said, "I don't know. That was an extremely awful and painful experience to go through."

Without missing a beat, he launched into me. Not with a sale this time but with my dream of a family. How bad did I want them? Why wouldn't I do it?

"Has your end goal of being a mother changed?" he asked me.

"No." I knew that answer without hesitation.

"Then why wouldn't you do it?"

Then the officer manager chimed in. "Carrie, we want to be your champion for this dream. It's the smart thing to do. But this time, you really need to work on your mindset. I believe you ovulated early because you had a poor mindset."

Thankfully, the doctor cut her off from putting her foot in her mouth any deeper and pulled the conversation back to the two of us. He went into more details about this next round not being as taxing on me emotionally since his time was free, his office's time was free, and I still had sperm from the donor.

"I still don't have the money to cover the drugs, though," I reminded him. I couldn't afford another $6,000 of drugs.

I wouldn't acknowledge the office manager again, but out of the corner of my eye, I saw her lean forward in her chair to get my attention and say, "We know of an organization that gives out grants to women who need help paying for the drugs. You could fill out an application and get 25 to 75 percent of the drugs discounted."

While looking at the doctor, I thought of the number of breakdowns I'd had within the last month because of the cost of this journey.

Without meeting her gaze, I asked, "Why wouldn't you tell me that a month ago when we started this? The money caused me major distress, and that could have been avoided."

Silence.

"Get me the information," I said.

She left.

The doctor and I agreed to do a second round starting on Black Friday 2016 and completing a second retrieval the first week of December. This decision meant that the Grade-C embryo would go into storage, and whatever I was able to create with this second round would join it in December.

God help me, I thought. *I'm about to put myself through this shit a second time.*

I sat as still as possible, watching the doctor record our appointment in his notes.

I felt another bubble of possibility growing just outside my thoughts. I couldn't fully embrace it or grasp it yet. I wanted to but didn't trust it.

The door to his office opened and the office manager handed him a grant application for fertility drugs over my shoulder.

I expected to see an essay-writing section, but instead I only saw instructions to submit my yearly tax return and an overview of how much money I intended to make that year. If they thought I would be a good candidate for financial support, I would be invited to send in a written proposal. I had written hundreds of grant applications for Severson Sisters but never one that made a decision solely based on my financial status. I folded the application and put it in my purse. That single piece of paper could be worth $1,500 to $4,500.

December wasn't for several months so I would have time to decompress, address all the negative thoughts running amok in my head, and think about the slivers of possibility I felt from time to time. On the drive back to my house, I called my mom to fill her in on everything. I've always been able to feel and hear her emotions, and she takes everything that happens to me so personally. When I got back to my house, I dropped onto the couch and told my mom I needed to talk out some questions rolling around in the back of my mind.

"What if I go through a second round and ovulate early again?" I asked.

"That could happen."

"What if I don't get the grant?"

"I can't help you pay for this next round, so if you don't get it, you can't do it."

"So everything depends on the grant, then."

"Yes," my mom said.

"I think I'll do everything different this next round. I'll eat super clean. I won't work out. I'll just sleep as much as possible and meditate when I'm not sleeping. I won't work or worry about working. Everything will be different this round."

"So apply for the grant and let's see what happens."

"You think I should do a second round, though, right?"

I always wanted my mom to be on my side when I made huge life decisions.

"Yes."

When the grant application submission window opened, I applied.

I spent the next several months working on letting go of anger and blame and whatever guilt I felt for putting myself through this.

And then, one morning in November 2016, while standing in the checkout line at my neighborhood market, I felt my phone vibrate in my back pocket. I popped open the e-mail icon and saw an e-mail about with the subject line, *Your grant results.*

I couldn't get myself to open it. I tossed it inside my grocery basket, and without thinking about it, I cradled my belly with my free hand. It ached, but this time it ached for the possibility of what was yet to come. I was caught off guard. For months, I remembered the loss whenever I felt my belly and was filled with such mixed emotions of guilt and anger. But standing next to strangers who were waiting to pay for their weekly groceries, I felt hopeful.

I paid, packed up my car, and drove home. I was afraid to move too fast, drive too fast, turn on the radio, or inhale too deeply out of fear that the hopeful possibility would pass.

Once at home and in the kitchen, I pulled out some onions, celery, red potatoes, and carrots and placed them in the sink. I turned on the water and watched it fill up for a few moments. I pulled out my wooden cutting board and best chopping knife.

My phone buzzed on the kitchen table behind me. It was the e-mail notification again. I still couldn't get myself to look at it. I wanted to keep that feeling of peace, of serenity. I knew in that moment that all was well within my soul. In that moment, I wanted to believe that the babies I would one day be a mother to were sparkles in the corners of my eyes. I wanted to think about how the man I was supposed to raise them with was out there chopping veggies for dinner, too.

My house was still and silent, with the exception of the knife hitting the wooden cutting board. There was something soothing and rhythmic about the sound as it echoed in my tiny kitchen.

I imagined the kids were playing in the next room and my husband was out for a run. He'd be home just in time for salmon, smashed red potatoes, and veggies. I turned the oven on and grabbed a baking dish, foil, and some garlic. There were four red potatoes in the sink ready for smashing. I sprinkled them with some fresh garlic, drizzled them with olive oil, and set the timer for thirty minutes. The salmon was waiting for me in a small dish on the stove. I cut off a block of butter and plopped it right on the top. A little dill followed. When they both went into the oven, my phone chimed again. Another e-mail notification.

This time I was ready to chance my hopeful bubble of possibility popping with the grant results. If I didn't receive funding, I couldn't do a second round. Before I grabbed my phone, I said a prayer and did a quick breathing exercise. With my feet hip-width apart, I envisioned a pretty pink ball of light just in front of me. With each inhale, it moved closer. With each exhale, it grew bigger. I imagined the bubble melting into my skin and then my cells. After another big, deep breath, I opened my eyes and grabbed my phone.

Dear Carrie,

We have reviewed the supporting documentation you provided, and you have been accepted for an additional 25 percent off . . .

An exhale of relief came first. The possibility was still there. I imagined the sparkles and the husband. He would be coming home from his run any moment. I put my phone down and went back to the kitchen to finish dinner.

I pulled out a pan and added olive oil to it. Carrots went in to sauté first. And then panic set in. Twenty-five percent gave me a break in cost, but that still meant I had to pay another several thousand dollars within the next few weeks.

Panic wasn't the feeling I wanted to go into this new round of possibility with. It was the exact opposite actually.

The onions went into the pan next. The veggies were left on low, and I poured myself some wine and grabbed my journal. At the top of a page I wrote, *How can I do this round differently?* Underneath it, I made a list of self-care actions I could think of that were all totally opposite of what I did the first time.

- *Do yin and restorative yoga.*
- *Take slow walks.*
- *Do a flash sale now to make some quick cash and then stop working for two weeks.*
- *Ask for a different technician.*
- *Ask for free samples from drug representatives or the fertility clinic.*
- *Use any leftover drugs from the first round.*
- *Take more baths.*
- *Meditate as long as possible.*
- *Don't write about the experience publicly until you're years past it.*
- *Ask a few friends to check on you.*

I tore the paper out and taped it to my cupboard.

The oven timer buzzed. I plated myself half the salmon, some smashed potatoes, and an extra big helping of veggies. I imagined plating three more and taking our seats around the kitchen table. It wouldn't be empty forever. I had told myself for years this was just a phase I was walking through.

That night, at my kitchen table, I savored the silence. It would not be silent forever.

I knew it.

Possibility hung in the air that night, and it was still there when I woke up the next morning. I made myself a coffee and glanced at the ten action items taped to my kitchen cupboard. I looked at the third bullet point. I had a month before Black Friday so I had a month to make as much money as possible to feel confident and comfortable taking two weeks off work. I had a month to make more money than I had ever made before so I could easily buy gifts for the holidays without putting more stress on myself.

After coffee, I meditated and let my mind move to an alternative state of being. I saw myself surrounded by a big, bright light. Chills ran up and down my body, and I felt safe, supported, and protected. I would ask God for images and messages to help me move forward that next month so I could support myself and my sparkles. Clients' faces came to mind. Names of master classes came to mind. Storytelling services I could offer came to mind. And when I came out of meditation, I journaled everything out and then went to work.

I reached out to clients I hadn't talked to in a while and made them an end-of-the-year offer. Several of them jumped at the opportunity. They paid and booked right away. I was a quarter of the way to my financial goal within a few hours of starting!

Next, I created a series of webinars and turned them loose on my writing support group. I got a few enrollments within minutes.

Over the next month, I did a flash sale on my storytelling e-courses and earned what I needed to move forward and feel comfortable.

When Black Friday 2016 finally arrived, I was cooler and more collected. I had a new technician. She was sweet and compassionate. Even her voice was softer than the previous tech's. We got along much better, too. While I was in the fertility clinic one day for the prep ultrasound, a pharmacy representative dropped off some samples. I took notice and asked her if she had any free samples of drugs around the office, and each time I saw her, she gave me more free drugs. That was new. She wanted to help me feel as stress-free as possible. The free samples she gave me brought the cost of the experience down another $1,000.

While round two felt different in a lot of ways, there were several similarities. My boobs grew another size, as did my waistband. And all my emotions expanded. In the same moment, I could cry and access anger and ecstasy.

The differences, however, were a blessing.

My body felt lighter.

My cravings were more aligned with fruit than French fries.

I didn't want to kick my landscaper in his balls whenever he did his job.

My parents were both in town this time around, and I had someone available to help me from start to finish.

And by day nine of round two, my body was ripe and ready to go. The technician gave me the last trigger shot, and I went home and waited for the Harvest.

The day of my appointment was smooth and went as easily as possible. I slept at my parents' house down the street the night before, and I rolled out of bed and wore my pajamas to my appointment. My mom drove me.

I knew the drill by this point. The doctor and I had a conversation about round two and our goal of eggs versus embryos.

My goal of creating possibilities of sparkles hadn't changed. We agreed to freeze 40 percent of any good eggs and turn 60 percent of my Harvest into embryos.

After our plan was finalized, I put my legs up in the stirrups. The nurse pulled my hair back and up into a net. She stuck my forearm with a needle and drugged me up.

"Count backward from ten."

I got to seven.

The nurse woke me up, and I looked around. My mom was sitting there.

"How many did he get?" I asked to anyone and everyone in the room.

"Thirteen eggs and eight were good. He is freezing three eggs and turning five into embryos," someone said.

"It worked?" I cried in disbelief and total relief.

"It worked," the voice from the corner said.

My mom stroked my hair while someone else put on my socks, panties, and pants. I was given some orange juice and a breakfast bar. I slowly sat up and drank a little bit of juice. The doctor popped his head in and congratulated me. He told me he'd be in touch in five days to talk about how the embryos progressed.

I slid off the table and groaned. I was so grateful for the pain this time. In my drugged-up fog, I knew I had made the right move for my future. The nurse walked with me to the car, helped load me into my mom's SUV, and buckled me in. She hugged me and wished me luck before shutting the door.

Since I was in and out of sleep the whole day, I don't remember much. At one point, my mom woke me up to give me soup and crackers. The next time I awoke, she was sitting in the chair next to me watching a Christmas movie. The drugs had worn off by bedtime, and I didn't mind crawling into my bed, cradling my belly, and giving thanks for a successful round two.

Over the next five days, I did everything on my list. I took slow walks. I did yin and restorative yoga. I ate healthfully. I didn't work for a minute.

I had been waiting for the call on the fifth day. It rang, and I saw the clinic's number. I picked up on the second ring, anticipating the best news. I prayed for five embryos I could call sparkly possibilities. I imagined the conversation over and over in my head. He'd for sure tell me all was well.

But as soon as I heard his voice I knew something was wrong.

He didn't waste any time sharing the heartbreaking news. "Carrie, I'm so sorry to tell you that the five embryos did not make it past yesterday," he said.

I could practically feel my heart crack open a bit more. I grabbed my chest. Instantly, hysteria took over every cell in my body. All I could get out was "How could this happen?"

He apologized again.

I did everything right.

I ate all the right things.

I did all the right things.

It wasn't enough.

They were gone.

I hung up and fell to the floor.

Chapter Thirteen

FUNCTIONAL HEALING

THIRTEEN THOUSAND DOLLARS.

One hundred seven shots.

Two dress sizes.

Two bra sizes.

One Grade-C embryo.

Three frozen eggs.

For weeks after that call, I couldn't feel anything. My smile was on, but my eyes were dead. I was afraid to connect to my spirit. I was hoping it'd all go away with time, but deep down I knew better. I couldn't forget about it or hope, pray, or meditate it away.

I had created a life so out of alignment with everything I wanted once before. I knew I had major healing to do, and to get there I'd have to walk through so much pain. My emotions were so shot, and my body felt like somebody else's. I wanted to forget the entire experience.

To get through Christmas and New Year's without falling apart every other minute, I plowed full speed ahead. Beneath the surface of everything hid layers and layers of tears and rage.

A few days into January 2017, I could not avoid the pain any longer. Healing waited for me like a patient parent waits for her child to calm down after a tantrum. I could feel it heavy on my chest.

I surrendered to it the morning I owed my parents my first reimbursement check. We had agreed on a dollar amount that I could add to my monthly budget and easily pay off. So I opened my eyes and rolled to my side. And the guilt and failure took over.

It felt as if it had crawled into my heart and down my skin, almost like a new identity to step into. I lay there for a while, unable to shake the feeling of failure. Instead, I went through the actions of a typical morning.

Shower.

Coffee.

Breakfast.

And when I saw my journal on the coffee table, I waited for inspiration. It didn't come. I called my mom and told her I'd be by soon to deliver her a check.

Not long later, I pulled up to my parents' house and walked in through the garage. The bell rang, and I heard my mom's voice from the kitchen.

"Hello," she said.

"Hi, Mom."

I walked into the kitchen and grabbed a pen from the junk drawer. I avoided eye contact with my mom and stayed focused on the task of beginning to pay back my parents. I could feel her watching me from the other side of the counter, and as I signed my name, tears started to form.

And finally, after weeks of holding back the floodgates, the dam broke. I couldn't stop sobbing. I gripped my belly and my heart. My breath was stuck somewhere between the two. My mom rushed over, grabbed me, and held me as I had my first major breakdown since it all had happened.

She held me for minutes as I cried. My skin crawled, my flesh felt hot, and my knees gave in. My mom tightened her grip around me.

Similar to my burnout journey, I knew there were a range of emotions and feelings to unpack. But standing there, being held up by my mother, didn't feel like the place to dig deeper. It was too much to heal in a day.

I forced myself to turn it off like a faucet. I sucked in a deep breath and got it to my rib cage. I exhaled and melted in her arms once more before rubbing her back.

"Thank you, Mom."

She released me and had tears in her eyes when she pulled away from me. I knew it was extremely hard on her, too.

I was numb the rest of the day. I crawled onto the couch with a blanket and fell asleep for most of the afternoon.

Within a few days, I was ready to face what was waiting for me. I grabbed my journal and turned inward. I started writing down words that came to mind:

Blame.

Betrayal.

Guilt.

Shame.

Embarrassment.

Irresponsible.

Selfishness.

Anger.

Fear.

Rage.

Hate.

Sadness.

Broke.

Journaling this way has always been a great way for me to move from one layer of existence to another. And blame was the lowest feeling I could access at the time, and I attacked it.

Dear Blame,

I hate that you're here. I hate feeling you so heavy on my heart. It would be so much easier to feel joy and hope instead of you. What am I supposed to learn from this painful experience? I know whom I blame and whom you are associated with and attached to.

I blame him. I blame his staff for their lack of understanding. I blame him for the drugs that put my body in such a state of stress that I ovulated early. I blame him for the loss

*of those five souls. I blame him for the cost of the procedure.
I blame him for the cost of the drugs.*

*I blame the drugs for the weight I'm carrying around. I
blame my career for having to do this in the first place.*

I blame myself most of all.

I called the fertility clinic and told the friendly technician that
I was upset I hadn't heard from them since the failed attempt.
I asked for the first available appointment with the doctor. I
wanted to know why it didn't work. Again. She understood the
need to talk about it, and she scheduled me for an appointment
later that week.

For the next few days, I journaled as much as I could around
blame and how I could move through it. Pages came pouring
out of me. With each new sheet of paper, my blame dissipated.
Rage and hate and anger came to the surface next. One by one,
I addressed each one, and I was able to put some emotional distance between the doctor and me by the time my appointment
came around later that week.

The truth of the matter was that the doctor was nothing more
than a man who happened to have a really weird job involving
sperm and eggs. He's not God. And if I were meant to be a mom, I
would still have that possibility. I knew that in the deepest part of my
heart, but at the time, I couldn't see it, feel it, or accept it. All I could
do right then, in that first step of moving out of my own despair and
deep depression, was to blame the man who had let me down and
feel the hatred and anger and rage against him and his team.

The morning I was scheduled to meet the doctor finally came, and when I showed up for my appointment this time, nobody greeted me. I didn't feel like a patient anymore; I felt like a case. After several minutes, the doctor came out to the front lobby to get me himself. There wasn't a handshake or a hug. He stepped aside, and I walked silently to his office. The technicians didn't look at me as I passed their desks. I didn't say hello. I marched into his office and sat down in the same chair I had sat in months earlier before any of this had taken place.

I assumed my defensive position. I pressed my fingernails into my palms, tightened my ass muscles, and curled my toes under. I was determined to keep eye contact. I was determined to hold back any tears. I was determined to tell him I was disappointed in him and wouldn't recommend him or his team to any woman I knew.

We sat across from each other, and he did what he did best: he talked to me about the science of it all. He showed me charts of five women he had worked with on the same week as me. I was the only one who'd had a bad outcome. He couldn't explain it. The embryos had evolved the way they were supposed to on days one, two, and three, and on day four their progress had slowed down and it had become obvious the embryos weren't going to make it.

And his only conclusion was that the sperm had been bad.

When I heard that, heat raced down my arms and into my sweating palms. I dug my fingernails into my flesh again to keep a straight face. My jaw clenched, and my tongue pressed against my front teeth.

The next thing he suggested was that I find a man and do it again in a year.

I couldn't think anymore. My hands were numb and clammy. I needed to get out of there and move on as fast as possible.

I stood up and walked out without saying anything or looking back.

Before I got to the door, I relaxed my still-fisted hands and pleaded to God to take my blame, hate, anger, and rage from me. I didn't want them following me home from that awful office.

When I drove away that afternoon, my body finally caved. It was six weeks to the day from my last injection, and I couldn't hold the tears back. They clouded my eyes and poured down my face. I could barely see the road. I pulled over and let everything rip through me like a wild and unpredicted storm. I couldn't control it so I just let it happen. I kept the car running and turned on the radio in case anyone walking by could hear me screaming.

By the time it passed, I was exhausted—and super snotty. I drove home, crawled into bed, and stayed there the rest of the day. When morning came, the emotional shitstorm had passed, but like all storms, what had been left in its wake was damaged. My body was wrecked, weak and achy everywhere. My head and sinuses pulsed. Even my eyes hurt. I could hear my heartbeat in my ears. I was sad and wanted nothing more than to stay in bed and go back to sleep.

My mom called to hear about my appointment.

"Did I wake you?"

"I've been up but still in bed. I don't feel well."

"You don't sound good. Can I bring you something?"

I rattled off some things I thought might make a shitty situation like this any better, and shortly after I'd hung up the phone, she was on my patio with a grocery bag. She had picked up my favorite chicken soup, crackers, some sort of cold medication, and ginger ale.

She took one look at me and said, "You look like you have the flu." She unpacked groceries and poured ginger ale into a glass for me.

It had been twenty years since I'd had the flu so I hadn't recognized it, but for the next ten days I hated life. I couldn't move, and when I did, I was afraid I'd vomit all over the place.

When it finally passed, I was ready to start working on the stress and weight that I had gained with the fertility treatment. I found a hot yoga studio and enrolled in an easy class. I told the instructor I was recovering from an internal battle and needed to sweat without doing much work. She blessed me and gave me a hug, so I found a spot in the corner and took a ninety-minute nap.

It was bliss. Every other morning for the next several weeks, I cried and rolled around in a hot yoga room. Hot yoga helped me reconnect to my intuition and get back in touch with the soulful parts of myself I felt so betrayed and hurt by. The more classes I went to, the happier I felt. After a few weeks, I felt comfortable and balanced enough to participate in a full class.

The light inside me slowly expanded with each day and each class.

And when March 2017 started, I assumed the sinus infection I'd come down with was just par for the course. That much sweating, crying, shedding, and change in such a short amount of time can't be good for anyone's sinuses. But when a nasty illness went around Phoenix a few weeks later, I caught that, too.

I had the same physician assistant at the doctor's that I'd seen for the sinus infection earlier that month, and he smiled when he saw me. "Oh wow! You're back."

I made a joke about not being able to stay away from the germ-infested incubator that was his office. He spent fifteen minutes checking me out and prescribed me the same antibiotic I'd taken last time.

Over the next two months, I caught two more bacterial infections and the flu for the second time in twenty years. With each illness, my spirit weakened. I had aged years within months. My body ached, throbbed, and overheated. Vertigo set in, and I couldn't walk down a hallway without feeling as though I was on a roller coaster.

Come May 2017, I was bedridden. I needed help getting from my bed to the bathroom and back to bed. On the good days, I'd make it to the couch, bathroom, kitchen, and bed all by myself. It'd take me three times as long to walk from one place to the other than it used to, but I did it!

The antibiotics my doctor and her team had given me time and time and time and time again finally led to a bacterial infection growing on my skin. It had started under my left boob and ran up and down my torso.

After the most recent flu and upper respiratory infection had passed, I went searching for a new medical team. By that point, my faith in the health-care system and medical community had flat-lined. I heard about a doctor with years of experience and her own functional medicine practice. At first it felt like a big weight had been lifted from my gut, which had grown by another dress size. My stomach was hard and distended, and reminded me of my failed fertility treatments.

My first appointment at the functional medicine office lasted hours. We sat across from each other with nothing between us. It was informal and vulnerable. She opened the session by warning me that some of her questions were going to be incredibly personal but that it was vital that I answer them honestly.

My shoulders tightened, and my butt cheeks clenched.

Her first question to me was, "What was your birth experience like?"

My birth experience?

I looked at her and waited for the real question to come.

She just nodded.

"I guess it was good?" I said cautiously. "I made it."

I was born on a Monday morning in July. I'm a Cancer with a Sagittarius moon rising. There's some Leo in there, too. My parents didn't have a car seat when they left the hospital, but it was the seventies. Apparently nobody had car seats when they left the hospital. I lived. It was fine.

I gave her the few details I knew, and we spent the next two hours in this intense Q&A about moments in time I hadn't thought about for years. She asked about old boyfriends and terrible breakups. She asked about my years being bullied and depressed. She asked about fads, trends, tricks, and tools I had tried over the years to shed weight and embrace stress, and about the different supplements I took.

Finally, we got to the fertility treatment—both rounds of it. The doctor raised her eyebrows, and they stayed like that the entire time I was talking. After going through the grotesque details of the hemorrhage, painkillers, and soaked pads, I told her about the five embryos that didn't make it.

The energy in the room changed. I felt it in my belly. She stopping typing and looked up from her computer. She handed me a tissue box.

Despite the fact that I had already cried so many tears—and sweat, and shed, and changed so much—talking about the fertility loss brought me to my knees. I was paralyzed with pain and sorrow, and all I could do was let it pour out of me into piles of tissues.

Sorrow. It was the emotion I hadn't been able to access until that moment. My body had been peeling back emotions through all the illnesses, but I couldn't feel them until I sat across from a woman who was questioning everything.

The doctor sat in silence and let me have the time I needed to get out whatever clearly needed to come out. When I calmed down and could breathe normally again, she asked me for the names of the drugs I had been on. I was able to recite them all without any trouble. And when that was done, she asked me if the fertility trauma was what had brought me to see her.

Trauma.

My fertility experience *was* traumatic, and it had taken two rounds of influenza and five bacterial infections for me to recognize that.

I listed off the illnesses I'd had to fight off since the second round of IVF. I pulled up my T-shirt and showed her the rash that had started to spread up my torso.

It felt more like a therapy session than a doctor's appointment, and I left that first session hopeful that I had found my loophole out of the traditional health-care system. I also left with a bill for $300, a urine test that cost just as much, a stool test that cost $200, a blood test order that included fifty-five different codes, and an armful of supplements I had been instructed to start taking right away.

The next day I peed in the cup and sent it off to the laboratory. The stool test required that I collect samples over a three-day period, so I did what I had to for the first day. Gratefully, I was able to get right in at a clinic to have my blood drawn.

The woman at the lab took my order and told me it'd be a few minutes to get the room prepared for me. She handed me a bottle of water and advised me to drink it as fast as I could while I waited. I finished the bottle as the technician called my name to follow him back to the office. I laid my purse down and took my seat. He had twenty vials laid out next to the chair. Before we could begin, I had to approve the labeling on every vial.

After I approved the first few vials, it hit me. I was really ill. I had taken action to preserve my fertility and now I was questioning if I'd made a mistake.

Was it IVF that made me ill?

By the time I was reading the twentieth label, I could barely see. The tears made their way to the surface, and I couldn't keep them captive any longer. I nodded my head for the twentieth vial, and in exchange, the technician handed me the tissue box.

"I'll wait," he said.

I sobbed into a tissue and pressed my fingertips against my eyes in hopes that it would make the crying stop. It didn't work.

He stood across from me. "We have some time here," he said. "It'll take a while to fill all twenty. We can talk about it if you want. You're not the first person to have a meltdown in that chair. It happens every day."

He was sweet and started making jokes about a television series he wanted to create called *Secret Stories in the Lab.*

Laughter is a great tool, and I let him make me laugh. The crying subsided, and my breathing calmed. I held my arm out for him, and we began.

After ten minutes, all twenty vials were filled, and I thanked him for his time. I wanted to hug him, but it felt unprofessional or maybe cliché after hearing about how often that room was used as a therapy office.

It took five days for the blood work to come back. My doctor called with the results. The panel showed that my immune system was pretty broken.

My cortisol level was four times higher than average.

My adrenals were on the fritz.

My glucose and insulin levels were messed up.

Vitamin B, C, D, and DHEA weren't even measurable.

I also had grown an aggressive yeast infection in my gut called candida overgrowth.

When the urine and stool results came back a few weeks later, the doctor was able to see two additional fungal infections in my belly. The good news was now I had answers and a game plan. I had to rebuild my immune system, which was going to take some time. And while I was doing that, I had to kill off a bitch of a yeast infection in my gut.

The doctor prescribed a number of supplements and a high-dose antifungal to help me kill the candida. She also suggested I lean on my family over the next several months, as I was going to feel much worse before the dawn broke. She warned me about fatigue, headaches, diarrhea, body aches, chills, and mood swings.

But there was something else I had to know before I hung up the phone with her.

"Do you think this is all because of the fertility drugs?" I asked her.

She suggested that the stress my body was under during that time was tremendous and clearly something broke my immune system. But she couldn't say with one-hundred-percent certainty that in vitro fertilization was the straw that finally broke the camel's back. She reminded me that healing my body was the important focal point now. And there was only one place I could think to go to heal my broken body. I had healed there once before.

Two days later, with a small duffel bag filled with medications in tow, I boarded a plane to Wisconsin.

Chapter Fourteen

RESHAPING SELF-LOVE

REPAIRING MY BODY WAS MY TOP PRIORITY. MEDICAL EXPERTS may not have been able to tell me with confidence that the rapid decline of my health was directly related to my fertility treatments, but I was convinced it had been the trigger in my case.

Similar to my last trip back to my childhood home, I didn't plan my return to Phoenix. I had a one-way ticket to Wisconsin and didn't worry about anything but getting on the plane.

This time around, I didn't have to notify a team of people about my plans. The nonprofit had been closed for a year at that point, and I had my own business as a storytelling coach. I could work from anywhere. I had clients around the world, and our calls were always on a video conference. They didn't care where I held our calls as long as I showed up and could support them. Still, I gave myself a few weeks without client calls so I could adjust to my new routine.

Ironically, the timing of my trip home was almost identical to the timing of my burnout recovery. This time, I arrived home one day after my thirty-ninth birthday. It was four years later, and I was right back where my first soul quest started.

This was a soul quest I couldn't see through. I didn't try. There was so much head fog, pain, and inflammation running through my body, I couldn't think about anything but the present moment. I had never been one to really know how to be peacefully in the "now" so it took some getting used to.

I unpacked my checked bag in the bedroom I had grown up in. I put my panties, socks, and bras away in the same drawer they had been assigned twenty years before. My yoga pants and sweatpants were in the same drawer, as well. When I was done putting my clothes away, I looked at myself in the mirror and had a flashback of the morning of my thirty-fifth birthday. Burnout meant something different to me this time around. There was more grace in the room. I could feel it. I just didn't know how to accept it.

Getting up and down the stairs wasn't easy. I went slow and leaned again the wall as I moved. I had brought a bag back with me filled with things from the doctor, and I unpacked that in the kitchen. I laid out thirteen bottles of medications and supplements on the counter. My pillbox had seven columns, one for each day of the week, and four rows per day to allow for breakfast, lunch, dinner, and bedtime. I twisted the caps off all my medications and supplements, counted out the twenty-six little pills I had to take every day, and dropped them into the little compartments in my pillbox.

The breakdown looked like this:

- Eleven supplements and two different medications in the morning.
- Twelve supplements to take between meals to help lower my cortisol and kill off the candida.
- Three supplements before bed to lower my cortisol again and help me digest everything.

In addition to feeling like a walking pill dispenser, I read everything I could about killing off candida overgrowth, and I changed my diet on day one of this recovery. It wasn't that I was eating poorly to begin with, but I had to cut out all fruit, all root veggies, everything that had anything remotely close to sugar in it, and all things that tasted good and comforting. So not only was I willingly walking back into a traumatic experience but I was doing it without comfort food. No mac and cheese for me. No faux mac and cheese, either. No gluten-free bagels, bread, or muffins. No soy. I had to heal everything with eggs, spinach, tomatoes, onions, garlic, zucchini noodles, and meat.

The first week was the most challenging as I searched for a new rhythm and new recipes.

Every morning, as soon as I opened my eyes, I scanned my body. Headaches, body aches, and body weakness were usually right there waiting for me to start my day. I knew by the time I walked to the bathroom if it was going to be a day I'd have to spend on the couch or not. When the die-off of the yeast, fungus, and bacteria overgrowth was particularly bad, my legs felt like concrete. I couldn't move them fast, if at all. The throbbing that shot up and down them brought me to tears and made it hard to walk. Headaches lasted days. And at night, I experienced terrors that made me scream out loud and throw things across the room.

The night terrors were really bad when my pain level was high. One morning I woke up to find my night lamp shattered on the floor across the room. A few pillows and a sock lay next to it. I was grateful I could only remember bits and pieces of the things that woke me up at night.

Even though sleep meant the possibility of scary dreams, the only thing that really helped during that first month was napping and hot baths. Napping became my newfound indulgence. There was something secretive and feminine about it. I was in the dark, under layers of comfort, and the rest of the world was busy keeping it spinning. I'd set an alarm on my phone to wake me up in time to take the next dose of medication, and then I'd go right back to sleep.

By the end of August 2017, I was able to recognize that the emotional pain from my in vitro fertilization experience was less present. It was replaced with a willingness to forgive and let the emotional trauma be something that didn't take over my life but simply passed through it. When a wave of grief would hit me, I'd fold into it and feel it.

To make sure that my coaching business stayed alive during this recovery stint, I never scheduled calls in the morning and I stacked Monday, Wednesday, and Thursday afternoons. The more relaxed I became about my business, the more business came my way. I took the attention off my need to make money and put it on my body, fixing my immune system, releasing the trauma left over in my cells from the fertility treatment, and loving myself through the unfamiliar and uncomfortable moments so that I could become a better version of myself.

I was on my way of becoming Carrie 3.0 by the time fall officially hit in Wisconsin.

There's something about the seasonal change of summer to fall in Wisconsin that always inspired me to be outdoors. On the days I felt clear and free from aches, I'd go for walks around a nearby pond. It took me twenty-five minutes to walk a mile, and I'd celebrate each step. When I felt really strong, I took a second lap around the pond. That next lap was a sensory practice I created for myself. There was a bench on the path I walked on, and I sat down to meditate. With my eyes open, I imagined my body filled with bright, gold light. I focused on my breath and pictured tree roots coming out of my feet and running down deep underground. I took the time to look at the trees reflecting on the water and the sunbeams dancing on the waves. I searched the skies for hawks and the ground for squirrels. I'd put my energy on my ears and listen to as many types of birds as I could, the leaves around me, and even the splashing of the water up against the rocks.

The slower I went, the more connected to my body I felt. And that second lap around that pond became my goal every day.

One day, on my second lap, a new sense of hope caught hold of me. I hadn't yet found solace from the five lost embryos, but what was clear to me was the gift the whole experience had provided. It hadn't been a mistake. It may not have been the Plan B and Plan C that I'd originally gone into that decision with, but the gift was there all the same.

It was easy for me to see that this soul quest was bringing me face-to-face with a version of myself I hadn't met before. I was in the most real, self-loving relationship with myself I had ever known. And I didn't just like who I was becoming. I loved her, loved me. I craved to get to know her more, me more. What made her tick, this new Carrie? How could I let that Carrie out more?

Enough with the old ways of being. I was ready to embrace the new. I sat there on the bench thinking about all the ways I could allow her more space.

I could feel my heart expanding. I wondered if I had ever loved myself, *really* loved myself, before that moment.

The term *self-love* flashed through my mind. I knew what *self-care* was all about. I was pretty good at that. But how could I shape what *self-love* meant to me as my body and heart were being molded into something new?

I thought about all the ways I had taken care of myself in the past. I had been so good about sticking to my nonnegotiable list years before. I'd made myself a priority as I recovered from burnout. I'd played in the ocean. I'd gone to dance classes. I'd visited friends. I'd created a deeper connection to my spiritual self. I'd celebrated God. I'd taken care of myself. I'd eaten healthier and paid my bills. I did self-care well.

When I thought about self-love, I thought about the dinners and movies I sometimes treated myself to. I thought about the hair salons, massages, pedicures, personal trainers, extra scoops of ice cream, or any indulgence that made its way into an online cart.

Most things I associated with self-love involved another person pampering me because I thought I deserved it. It was clear

I had tied money and worth to self-love. It usually involved *doing something*.

Pampering myself wasn't something that belonged in the self-love column. I didn't really know what self-love meant.

What does it mean? I thought to myself.

I took my time on the bench that day, just watching the clouds go by, waiting for answers to emerge. I thought back to how else I'd recovered from burnout those four years prior. I had recreated what success meant to me through journaling and mindset exercises.

Before my burnout, success had meant being recognized with awards and money. Now, after my burnout, it's about being truthful with my voice and acknowledging myself for who I am in each day and how I show up in the world that day. A successful day post-burnout is marked by feeling happy, knowing I am loved by God, and feeling connected with myself and with a bigger life force all around me. I feel successful when I share openly about things I'm passionate about, knowing that the Universe will guide my message to anyone who needs it. Success isn't attached to my career anymore. It stems from within me, and I project it in whatever I feel like doing.

I took a deep breath and smiled at the ducks drifting along the edge of the pond. Out of the corner of my eye I noticed some sort of critter pop its head above the ground. It disappeared just as quickly. And within seconds, a big black shaggy dog, soaked from enjoying a dip in the pond, came running up to me. He had a smile on his face, which made me giggle. His tongue hung out of the corner of his mouth, and he kept on trotting. I looked around and saw a woman down the path with a walking stick. When she passed me on the bench, she laughed and warned me that he'll most likely visit me again.

I was so preoccupied by the big shaggy dog running around the pond that I didn't get any more intuitive nudges that day. I enjoyed the sights, sounds, fresh air, sunshine, clouds, and time alone with God on a bench.

I stood up, took the deepest inhale I could, reached up to the sky, smiled, and exhaled while reaching my fingertips as high as they'd go. I thanked God for the talk and turned to head back to my car just in time for the shaggy dog to make his way out of the pond again. He saw me and trotted toward me, his tongue hanging out to the side again. He circled me twice, changed directions, and walked alongside me on my way to the car. I saw him jump back in the pond as I pulled away.

A few weeks later, I was rummaging through a drawer in my childhood bedroom and found a journal I had left behind from my burnout recovery four years prior.

To read how different my life was and how different *I* was from the Carrie who had run herself to the point of utter exhaustion hurt my heart. I sent that version of myself a big hug and exhaled.

And then an idea came to me.

I grabbed a pen and turned to a brand-new page.

October 29, 2017

What does self-love mean to me right now?

It means I care for my body, and she craves restoration and rejuvenation. I know that can happen through rest and sleep.

It means I crave a deeper connection to my own intuition, and I know I can get that through the stillness and silence that comes to me during my meditations. I love how I feel during and after meditation, and I love myself for giving myself these breaks in time and space.

It means I'm aware that I'm super supported by the Earth. When I take steps on its surface, I love myself at the deepest level possible. I'm aware of the support I have, and I'm capable of absorbing that support.

From that day forward, I made sure to ask myself at least once a day what self-love meant to me.

November 10, 2017

What does self-love mean to me today?

Self-love is a sense of being. I am a divinely made woman. Loving myself is a reflection of my love for God. And I think it's a reflection of His love for me. It means I listen to my heart. I trust myself and my journey. It means I love each cell in my body and actively imagine my body releasing inflammation. It means I trust that what I'm doing for my body will help me shed the poison still trapped within me. It means I love and care for myself so much and I know my purpose here is to have the best experience possible.

It was easier to praise my newfound appreciation for being unapologetic about my self-love on the days I felt clear of yeast die-off or trauma. On the days my legs didn't work or felt like hundreds of pounds of concrete were attached to them, it was nearly impossible to recognize that I was already practicing self-love by simply being in my body.

By December, there were many more good days than bad. My pain substantially subsided, and I could think more clearly. The number of medications I was on lessened, and I was able to reduce the supplements, too. The lighter I felt, the easier it was for me to use my voice as a storyteller again.

Some days that simply meant wearing makeup and taking a picture of it. Other days that meant recording what I was experiencing. The more I expressed myself and where I was in life, the more aligned I felt with my own voice. There was a new level of freedom and clarity in my expression.

I found ways to use my journey in my business when it felt right. I offered workshops and programs about trusting intuition and listening to our inner voices. The more open I was about what 2017 put me through, and the less I promoted myself, the more women came forward and asked to work with me.

December 8, 2017

What does self-love mean to me today?

It means I take deep breaths that feel so good. I can inhale the crisp air and exhale everything that ruined my immune system with every breath.

It means I acknowledge my body. She is a brilliant piece of magic. I am divinely made. She has just gone through some crazy, painful moments, and I am so proud of her.

She is strong. She is feminine. She is flesh and cells and freckles and curves and perfection. I am strong. I am feminine. I am flesh and cells and freckles and curves and perfection.

It means I acknowledge the need for a journal and give myself some time to write in it. I'm a talented, soulful writer. I'm able to shred old mindsets through my journal. I love myself when I take pen to paper and let my thoughts pour out without hesitation. Magic happens when I have aha moments in my journal. I feel lighter and it's easier to hear my own thoughts when I journal.

By the end of 2017, I'd made a big decision. I knew I would have to go back to Phoenix eventually since I had a furnished home with many belongings, but during that second recovery stint in Wisconsin, I had fallen back in love with the state and wanted to stay for good. I started to explore where I would live. What town could I see myself in? What networks should I join?

For the first time in a long time, I didn't just feel grounded, hopeful, and supported. I felt excited. I felt healed. I was in a much more peaceful place about my fertility treatments and felt whole again.

I called two girlfriends and told them I was thinking of moving back. Their reaction to my idea was so heartwarming. It felt like home and helped me to know for certain that I was moving in the right direction.

The three of us decided to meet up the following night for dinner. We talked about the unique roads that we had each taken in life, and we talked about what more we each wanted from life. They were both moms and married. They both loved their jobs. Our lives were so different. But I didn't feel a longing for what they had. I wasn't comparing our lives.

The desire to have a family and children still existed within me, but for the first time in a long time, I didn't have an attachment to it. If I was meant to have a partner in life, I would. If I was meant to have children, I would.

Instead of feeling deflated because of the journey I had been on, I felt triumphant. I was proud. I could finally see myself as a warrior. I saw the soul quests I had walked through as battle scars. I was in love with my life, and the woman I had grown into was capable of so much more than I had been allowing her to experience.

I shared my feelings with my childhood friends, and they both encouraged me to date while I was still in town. So right there at dinner I downloaded a dating app and started swiping right.

On the drive home that night, I was eager for my next chapter to begin. It wasn't just a physical move I was craving, I wanted to share how I had come to understand and appreciate my God-given right to feel loved within every cell of my being.

It became clear to me that I had conquered the path of reclaiming my voice and redefining what success and self-love meant so that I could help others do the same.

The next day I booked a ticket back to Phoenix. I had two weeks left in Wisconsin and used every minute I could to soak up the wonderful winter and even go on a date!

It was the first date I had been on all year, and it felt right to close 2017 with attention on my love life.

We met for a cocktail at a bar down the street from where I'd grown up. I laughed and enjoyed his company, and went on my way. The spark wasn't there, but I felt absolutely seen and heard.

Before I packed up my life to migrate back to Phoenix, I created one more round of soul contracts to help keep this unapologetic voice in place and call in support and direction in my life. This time, I made ninety-day soul contracts with my heart, my career, and my money.

I named myself the CEO of my own life. I gave my heart the title of Chief Heart Officer (CHO). My career was named my Chief Story Officer (CSO). The Chief Financial Officer (CFO) was assigned the title to represent my money.

The agreement I made with my heart went like this:

A Ninety-Day Contract Between CEO and CHO

I, Carrie Severson, declare love, light, and fun overflow in my life for the next ninety days. I give my love life over to my Chief Heart Officer to run with full responsibility.

My CHO calls in heart-centered men to have loving conversations and adventures with. I have heart-centered relationships show up on my path daily.

I agree to say yes to dates! I say yes to networking events and fun nights out with friends where I could potentially meet new people. I am easily introduced to new men who become friends and partners through my CHO. I agree to create a profile on dating websites, and my CHO attracts the right men to my life.

I go on two dates a month for the next ninety days and have the time of my life.

I have monthly meditation sessions with my CHO to talk about our progress and redirect as necessary.

My heart is full and alive. My CHO calls in my best friend and soul mate, and I trust my heart and CHO.

Signed,
Carrie Severson

It felt strong.

I felt strong.

And when the time came to board a plane to head back to Phoenix, I knew I'd be back. I had a return ticket to Wisconsin in April. I figured that gave me plenty of time to move.

Christmas came and New Year's went by, and nothing truly monumental had happened in my life. I kept my suitcase in the corner of my bedroom as a reminder that I wasn't staying much longer. And to keep energy flowing to and from my love life, and to keep aligned with my CHO contract, I looked at the dating app and swiped right now and again.

There weren't many men in Phoenix I was interested in seeing romantically, which was fine considering I was going forward with my plans to move back to Wisconsin. But to stay open to love, I followed through with my CHO contract. I went to networking events and met friends out.

Between getting rid of belongings and furniture, and searching for a place to live in Wisconsin, I agreed to go out with a man named Gavin.

The night before our date, he sent me a text to confirm when and where we were meeting. And he ended it with a happy face, kiss emoji, and his name. *That's different.* It was refreshing not to see the eggplant and tongue emojis.

We met at a bar halfway between our homes on a Friday in March. I picked my favorite pair of jeans, a dark-blue tank top, and a cardigan. I picked a neutral lip gloss, swiped the mascara wand across my eye lashes twice, and put on three gold bangles and a rose quartz pendant. I wore flats because I knew he wasn't much taller than me. I knew he was divorced. I knew he had children. And I knew he had spent time in the financial industry.

I saw him sitting at the bar. He had saved the seat to his left for me. He watched me walk toward him, and he pulled the chair out for me, leaned in, and gave me a kiss on my cheek.

Our date was easy and comfortable. We talked about hobbies, our career paths, where we had grown up, his divorce having been finalized just a few months prior, and movies. After a little while, he asked if I'd like to go see a movie with him.

"Sure, that would be nice."

I listed off a few movies I'd like to see, and he checked times at the closest theater. He called the bartender over, paid our bill, and asked me if I was ready to go.

"Oh, you mean go to a movie now?"

"Yes. I'm not ready for the date to be over. Are you?"

I smiled and shook my head. He grabbed my hand as we walked to his truck, and it felt like we had been doing that all along.

There was something safe and familiar about Gavin, but I didn't read much into it that night. He kissed me goodnight at the end of the date and asked me to meet him again for St. Patrick's Day, the following weekend. We texted throughout the week leading up to our second date.

We agreed to meet at a bar in Scottsdale that was throwing a St. Patrick's Day party. He got there before I did and gave me a casual wave when my eyes found his. I couldn't help but smile. He pulled me close to him, hugged me, and kissed me on the cheek. I put my jacket and purse on the bar, and Gavin handed me a green beer.

"Cheers," he said.

My grandpa would have loved him.

We launched into conversation about our weeks and what we both knew about our Irish heritages.

This man *saw* me. And when he put his hand on the small of my back to lead me out of the bar, I felt unapologetically supported. His touch was gentle. It was safe. We made our way through the crowd, him in front of me. He reached his hand out behind him, and I placed mine in his and smiled.

He held my hand as we bobbed and weaved past the other par-tygoers, as if we would have lost each other in the one hundred feet from the door of the bar to the sidewalk.

We stayed linked together as we meandered through the men and women out enjoying the celebration. My stomach did flips, and butterflies flew all around inside it all day long.

My love language is quality time and I guessed his was touch, so I figured we were both in our happy places by the time the sun set on our St. Patrick's Day date.

At some point between meeting Gavin and the end of that date, I knew he was the man I was going to call my husband one day. The plans I had for moving back to Wisconsin dissipated in my heart but not in my mind.

Chapter Fifteen

THE LOVE BUBBLE

MY PHONE BEEPED ON THE COFFEE TABLE, WAKING ME UP
from a nap. It was a text from Gavin.

*Hi, Carrie. I had a great day with you yesterday. *Cool sunglass
guy emoji face. Kissy lips emoji.**

Me too! It was so much fun, I texted back. *Blushing emoji face.*

When can I see you again?

*Do you want to come to my house for appetizers, and we can see if
we want dinner somewhere down here tomorrow night?* I asked.

Perfect. What time?

How's 6:30 p.m.?

*See you then. *Kissy lips emoji.**

Kissy lips emoji.

I put my phone down on the coffee table and noticed my stomach was fluttering and my heart was buzzing. It could have been the green beer trying to make its way back up, but I was excited either way. I rolled into the cushions and pressed my forehead into a heating pad I had draped over the back of the couch.

My phone beeped again not long after. It was my mom. I knew before I picked up that she wanted to talk about my date. As the only child of hers who was not married, my love life was always a big, bright, neon-pink elephant in the room. Sometimes it felt like that elephant was doing cartwheels through the center of the damn room and other times she was sitting quietly in the corner waiting to come out. But she was always there.

"Hi, Mom," I said.

"Did I wake you?"

"No, I'm just on the couch with a hangover."

"So how'd it go with Gavin?" she asked.

"We had a lot of fun," I said.

"That's good! Where'd you go?"

I listed off a few bars we had spent time at. I talked about walking around Old Town Scottsdale and topics we'd discussed.

"We both had a lot of green beer. We took a cab back here, and we both passed out. I took him back to get his truck really early this morning," I said.

"Are you going to see him again?"

"We made a date for tomorrow night."

"I'm so glad for you, honey!"

It was rare for me to share details of dates with my family. I did what I could to hide my dating life from them for the most part. It was easier that way since relationships hadn't worked out for me before and everyone was always heartbroken with me when they ended. That usually made it harder for me to move through my own pain and I'd feel worse.

In the past, when they would find out about men I was dating, the pressure to invite my boyfriend to meet them usually came on months before my peers' parents asked to meet their special someone. My parents would ask to meet my dates for brunch or some holiday dinner. Special plates came out along with my grandma's silver. It was a big deal. They were raised that way, though. We, as a whole, can be intense. Even though my immediate family was just my sister, brother, parents, and me, my extended families were huge. Holidays weren't held at one person's home. We had to rent out halls and centers. Everyone knew everyone's business. One person called a sibling, and before long, cousins and second cousins knew things. It's usually a blessing, but when it came to romance and the men in my life, the fewer people who knew the specifics, the better.

The only reason my mom knew about Gavin at that point was because she had been in the car when he'd sent me a text one day before our St. Patrick's Day date and she had seen my reaction.

"Who is that from?" she'd asked.

"Nobody," I had said quickly.

"Why are you smiling, then?"

I hadn't responded.

"It's not nobody. Who's it from?"

So I told her. It had just been easier to let her know I'd met someone than hide him.

Before I hung up with my mom that Sunday afternoon, she wanted to make sure I was coming over for dinner. Sunday dinners were a staple in both my parents' upbringings. It was something I was raised with, as well. Since I lived down the street from my parents', if I didn't have plans on Sunday, I was at their table. My sister lived in town with her husband, and they would come for dinner often, along with any relatives or friends who were in town visiting.

"Yes, I'll see you later."

After my conversation with Mom, I turned off my phone and pulled a blanket up to my chin in the hope that a nap would erase my headache.

A few hours later, the sun peeked through my blinds, which meant it was close to setting. I jumped in the shower to wash away the leftover grogginess and headed to Sunday dinner, wondering if my dad now knew about my date. And more importantly, if he knew Gavin had spent the night.

I walked into my parents' house, and my dad was in front of the grill already. My mom had laid out crackers, cheese, veggies, and dip on the kitchen counter. It was just us three for dinner, and that was fine with me.

I popped a piece of cheese in my mouth and dunked a stalk broccoli in the dip as my dad came in with a platter of food. We plated up grilled chicken, veggies, and pineapple, and sat down at the dining room table to pray.

"In the name of the Father, the Son, and the Holy Spirit, amen," we said together and then went into the prayer I learned as a young child.

Nothing was said about Gavin or my date at dinner. I could tell my mom wanted to talk about him, though. We cleared the table, loaded the dishes into the dishwasher, and put away the leftovers. My dad turned on his Sunday night show, and I went into my mom's pantry for one of our recipe binders.

For years, whenever my mom or I found a recipe in a cooking magazine that sounded good, we would put it in a binder. By that point, we had three binders filled with recipes. They were organized by ones we loved, stained with blotches of who knows what, and there were notes in the margins. We had one binder just with holiday recipes and a third binder with appetizer, brunch, and dinner recipes we still had to try.

I grabbed the binder of recipes with blotches and notes on it and curled up in one of the chairs in the family room, next to my mom. She smiled at me.

"I invited him to my house for dinner tomorrow."

"What do you think you'll make?"

"I'd like it to be really causal so I was thinking of just doing a handful of appetizers."

Mom grabbed the binder of appetizers we hadn't tried to make yet, and we spent some time pulling out recipes that sounded good. I left later that evening with recipes for prosciutto phyllo pinwheels, stuffed mushrooms, mini meatballs, and two new mini dumplings I could try if I wanted to be adventurous.

I went about my Monday morning as if nothing in my life had changed and I wasn't already in love with a man who lived in Arizona. Instead, I went for a two-mile walk around my neighborhood. I e-mailed clients and spent some time thinking up new ways to support women on their journeys to uncovering their own unapologetic voices. Later in the day, I climbed into my big, oversized chair and went inward to meditate. By four o'clock I'd decided on the prosciutto pinwheels, mini meatballs, cheese, grapes, and Marcona almonds. I had two hours to tidy up, put my suitcase in the closet, and buy groceries. As I rolled my suitcase into my closet, I thought about Wisconsin. Even though I'd never felt this way about a man before, I was all too familiar with getting excited over someone only to have it fall apart. And I knew I could easily talk myself into letting him go to pursue a plan I'd already created in a different state.

I pushed my suitcase behind my clothes and shut the closet door before any more thoughts came in. I grabbed my keys and wallet and set out to my corner market.

Gavin sent a text to confirm our date as I was checking out of the store.

See you soon. *Happy face emoji.*

Yep! I'm just grabbing some things at the store. Do you like wine?

I'll have whatever you're having.

I sent him my address and got a thumbs-up in return.

The ingredients to make mini meatballs stayed on the counter, along with one package of the frozen phyllo dough. I placed the rest of the groceries in the fridge and turned on some instrumental music to get me into a feminine-energy state of mind.

Before I made the mini meatballs, I jumped in the shower. My hair always had a mind of its own. The more I messed with it, the more unruly it became. I toweled off, placed some clips in my hair to help it air-dry, and pulled on an oversized dress. It really looked more like a house coat than anything else, but it helps me with the mess of cooking, boob sweat, and cooling down from a hot shower all happening at the same time.

By 5:30 p.m. I was ready to start. The mini meatballs were first and always took me a bit longer than the recipe claimed because working with raw meat wasn't something that came naturally for me. I waited as long as I could to actually touch the meat. If I could get around it by mixing up the meat with spoons and chopsticks, I did.

Just do it. He'll be here soon. You have to touch it this time.

I mixed everything in a bowl and rolled out twenty meatballs. I placed the tray in the oven at 6:00 p.m. and exchanged my house coat for a pair of jeans and flirty blouse. I brushed my teeth, dabbed some concealer under my eyes, then swiped the mascara wand across my eyelashes twice and a lip gloss stick over my lips once. I left the clips in my hair until the last possible minute to avoid hanging upside down over a hot hair dryer.

The prosciutto phyllo pinwheels were simple. Roll out the pastry, brush mustard all over it, lay prosciutto strips on top of it, roll them back up, and cut them. I waited for Gavin to arrive before I put them in the oven. I sliced some cheese and set it on a platter next to crackers, red grapes, and almonds. When the meatballs were ready, I poured some red sauce in a soup pot and plopped all twenty meatballs down into the sauce.

Gavin knocked on my patio door a few minutes after six thirty, and I met him with a big, warm hug and quick kiss on the lips. He smiled and let out a little sigh.

"Stressful day?" I asked.

"Just happy to see you," he said.

I gave him another quick kiss on the lips because my heart felt like it. I told him to take a look around the place since he may not have remembered what it looked like. Green beer can do that.

He complimented me on my decorating style and said it was inviting and comforting. I poured us two glasses of wine and handed him one. He clinked glasses with me and winked as we both took a sip. He leaned in for another kiss.

I asked him to grab the cheese platter, his glass of wine, and take a seat on the patio. The pinwheels went into the oven as I poured some meatballs and red sauce into a bowl, grabbed forks and plates, and went out to join him.

The night was easy. We talked about his children, my work as a storyteller, his mom, dad, and step-mom, growing up as a single child, and my family. Eventually, we went back to speaking about his children. He showed me photographs on his phone and reminded me that he had three sons.

"I just want you to be aware of the fact that I have some baggage," he said.

He wasn't the first divorced dad I'd dated, but I appreciated the fact that he wanted to have a conversation about it all so early in our courtship.

"I wasn't expecting to get into a serious relationship already, and this feels like it could be one," he said.

I didn't know what to say so I grabbed his hand and leaned over to kiss him.

That night was the start of it. When he left, I really felt like I was in a relationship.

Gavin and I fell in love quickly. Neither of us had seen it coming. He was newly divorced, and I was set on moving back to Wisconsin. But I wanted to say yes to love. We had met three days after my ninety-day soul contract with my heart ended, and I don't believe in coincidences. I manifested him. He walked in right when I was ready to honor the woman I had become and my plan to create a brand-new life back in the Midwest.

When you want to hear God laugh, tell him your plans. My grandpa said that whenever I'd tell him about something big I had in the works.

I had already enrolled in networking groups in Wisconsin. My flight back was scheduled to leave on April 11, and I had already started to sell dishes, lamps, and small tables in my home.

Leaving Phoenix was always on my mind. It held a space in my energy field, right next to this man I already loved. And then somewhere between the plane ticket and Gavin were all the questions rolling around in my brain:

> *What do I tell him?*
> *When do I tell him?*
> *Should I really leave?*
> *Should I stay?*
> *What if it doesn't work out?*
> *What if he freaks out that I don't want to go?*
> *What do I say if he asks if I'm staying because of him?*

Questions about my future were there when he took me out for dinner, breakfast, to the movies, and while we watched game shows on the couch. The only solace I had from the what-ifs was during meditation.

It was the close to the end of March, and I knew I had to say something. I wanted to make a decision about where I was going. So one Saturday morning, I sent Gavin a text. *Hey, I could use a day trip up to Sedona. Want to join me?*

Let's leave in an hour. Great idea.

There. I had the whole day to say something.

I drove over to Gavin's house and parked on the street. He met me at the door, ready to go. We hopped in his truck, stopped for gas and drinks, and got on the highway to Sedona. On the drive there, Gavin talked about this one spot in Sedona where he loved taking his kids to go fishing. It was a place he held dear. It meant something for me, too. It's a magical little safe haven that allows me to get grounded and feel safe, supported, and connected. Even though the red rocks of Sedona aren't anything like the green grass and gigantic trees of Wisconsin, I always felt a deep sense of peace there.

The drive went by fast. We talked about road trips we'd both been on, summer vacation spots we'd loved as kids, places we would want to still experience, and what we dreamed of doing for ourselves later in life.

He took me to a restaurant he liked that made just about everything and anything under the sun. We both had sandwiches and fries, and got back in the car. We headed to his fishing spot, even though we didn't have fishing gear. I leaned back and enjoyed the scenery as the road twisted and turned. I watched the creek down below and felt loved. Not just by Gavin, either. I felt it within myself, too.

I had been craving this, waiting for this, and it was finally here.

After skipping rocks and doing a little hike at the place where he took his kids, we drove to a state park. It was packed with families. The creek was spotted with kids as they splashed all around us in the water. We took a seat next to the creek and leaned back to people watch. It was simple being with him— just being. I had plenty of opportunities to bring up the plane ticket but didn't. I was enjoying the moment. I let the love I felt for him, us, Sedona, and myself fill my chest, run down my torso, and into my legs, which dangled off the rocks and skimmed the water.

I've never been very good at capturing moments with my camera, but something hit me that afternoon. I wanted a photo of this man and me in a place that felt supportive and magical. Before I could say something, Gavin reached for my phone, opened up my camera, and leaned back into me for our first selfie. I laughed as he kissed my neck.

It was then that I realized I could go to Wisconsin more than once that next year while Gavin and I figure out our relationship. I didn't have to stay in either place until we were both certain. I didn't have to be in such a state of anxiety about it. Wisconsin was good for my soul. It helped me uncover new chambers of my heart during great transitions before. It would do it again. And whenever I gave myself some time there, amazing new blessings flooded into my life and business. I told my monkey mind to shut up, and I let my heart speak up.

"We should get going," he said.

We took our time walking back to his truck. I climbed in and promised myself I'd tell him once we got on the highway.

Sedona is lined with small streets, roundabouts, and stop-and-go traffic. Gavin decided to take the long way back to the highway to avoid getting stuck, and I watched the scenery again as he drove through canyons. It felt safe so I spoke up finally.

"Hey, I've been meaning to tell you that I actually have plans to go back to Wisconsin for a bit," I said.

Gavin glanced at me. "When do you leave?"

"Two weeks."

"How long are you going to be gone?"

"Three weeks," I said.

"Three weeks," he repeated.

"Well that's the part that I wanted to talk about. Before we met, I had actually planned to move back there."

Gavin didn't say anything. His eyes didn't leave the road as I told him of my grand plans of going to Wisconsin a few times that year.

"I love it there and it's really good for me, so I do want to go back. But I'd like to continue whatever we have here and see where this goes."

"Well I want you to do what's best for you, but I'd also like you to come back," he said with a laugh.

"Me too."

I reached over and squeezed his shoulder. He smiled. I couldn't tell what he was thinking. I didn't push it, though.

The energy in the truck felt a bit heavy.

We pulled into Gavin's garage, and I wasn't sure where to go.

"Want to order something from the Chinese place down the street?" he asked.

I felt my shoulders relax some. "That sounds great."

We picked our favorites, and he called in to place our order. He went upstairs to shower off the day, and I curled up in the corner of the couch to meditate and show gratitude to myself and to God for helping me through the stuckness I'd felt about Wisconsin. I knew I'd done the right thing. His golden doodle, Princess Leia, curled up next to me and sighed as I exhaled.

Gavin came downstairs, grabbed his keys out of the basket on his counter, gave me a kiss, and went to pick up our dinner.

He was gone just a few minutes, but it gave me enough time to decompress and feel into my heart a bit more.

After dinner, we climbed into his bed and agreed on a show. I started to fall asleep on his chest, and he must have sensed it by the way my breathing changed. He cradled my head and kissed the top of it. I could feel the pressure of his cheek on my head. I had found my partner, *and* I still longed to honor that unapologetic woman I'd become. They were both on my mind and in my heart as I melted into his chest and fell asleep.

We spent as much time together as possible those next two weeks. We found a rhythm. He showed me his favorite places. I brought him to mine. I worked from the corner of his oversized couch with Princess Leia at my feet.

There was a tug-of-war happening between my heart and mind. We felt so natural together and had fallen into a relationship really quickly. And yet, there were parts of myself I hadn't introduced him to and things we hadn't discussed. My spiritual practice was still hidden. I'd meditate before he woke, and I filmed my "Coffee with Carrie" morning videos to the storytelling groups I ran as early as possible because those tended to be emotional and spiritual and filled with insights into how to share personal pieces of our pasts with the public. I filmed videos I'd use to promote programs or services of mine to a larger audience against an empty wall of his home so nobody could tell where I was. My heart was fully in, but my head was reminding me this was happening way too fast.

The Sunday after our Sedona trip was perfect. We had breakfast at his favorite diner, took Princess Leia for a hike, and went swimming together. After our swim, I gathered my things and left for Sunday dinner at my parents'.

This time, my sister, brother-in-law, and their little boy were there. My mom wanted to talk about Easter. My brother was flying into town with two of his children, and we would have extended family there, as well. We needed to discuss the menu and who else was coming.

I knew it . . .

Our holiday binders were on the kitchen counter, and my sister and our mom had a few of our favorite recipes pulled out already. At this point, we didn't need the look at recipes; it was more of a tradition and to keep track of who was making what dish.

My sister was making her green beans with shallots, sherry wine, bacon, and almonds. My brother-in-law was making his apple pie. I was looking for a brunch recipe to make for us all to have before church when my mom said, "I'd like Gavin to join us."

Here we go.

"Mom, it's really early."

"You're spending a lot of time with him, Carrie. We'd like to meet him."

CHAPTER FIFTEEN: THE LOVE BUBBLE

Even though it appeared as though my dad wasn't paying attention to our conversation in the kitchen, I heard him shout over
the television in the next room, "Just ask him to come, Carrie."

And that was that. Everyone smiled at me.

"I'll ask him."

My heart clenched, and my stomach fell a bit.

The next day I called Gavin and invited him to Easter. I
warned him that there would be eleven of us and it could be a
little overwhelming.

He accepted without hesitation and asked what to bring. I suggested a bottle of red wine for my dad.

When Easter day arrived, every trigger I hadn't healed
popped up:

What if he doesn't come?
What if he breaks it off because this is too much?
What if they hate him?
*What if I can't be the woman I had planned to be in
Wisconsin here in this relationship?*

I hadn't been able to pinpoint or verbalize any of that, but it
came out in waves of emotions and tears. We were moving so fast. I
didn't text Gavin or even communicate with him at all that day. I left
it in his court. My phone was pretty close to me at all times, though.

It felt like a lot for me. I had to be a lot for him.

He arrived a little late and apologized about it. He wanted to see
his mom before coming over and had stopped at the grocery store on
the way to my parents' place. He hadn't known what wine to bring.

I met him at his truck and gave him a hug and a kiss when I saw him. He sighed again and smiled.

"Why do you do that when you see me?" I laughed.

"It feels better to be with you."

I kissed him again before going inside.

My mom was first to welcome him in. She gave him a hug. The introductions were one after another. My dad shook his hand, as did my brother, sister, and brother-in-law. He went around and met all the nieces and nephews next and then the extended family. It looked like he was taking it all in stride, and I could breathe a bit better by the time we sat down to eat that afternoon.

He reached over and gave my thigh a squeeze when the conversation turned to us.

After our meal, my sister brought out a game for a handful of us to play, and at the end of the night, I walked him to his truck.

"Thank you for coming," I said.

"I am grateful for the invite. You have a really great family," he said as he pulled me in for a hug and a gentle kiss goodbye.

I knew my family would want to talk about him once I got back inside so I waited in the driveway as he backed out to give myself a bit more time to process the introduction. It was the last time I had hoped to ever have to do that. And it felt really good.

A few days later, we were sitting at his kitchen table, when out of the blue he said, "I love you."

"What?" I said, smiling.

"I love you," he said louder. He smiled, too.

I paused.

"You don't have to say it back."

I wanted to really feel it deeper in my belly when I said those words to him. I took a deep breath but couldn't get it down into my gut. My breath was stuck in my chest. I giggled and leaned in closer to him. I practically spit on him out of pure excitement. My heart was beating fast, and angel bumps covered my arms.

"I love you, too," I said.

It had been years since I said those words to a man. It felt amazing to have that out in the open. We couldn't take it back. He pulled me into him and kissed me.

It wasn't long after exchanging *I love yous* that I left for Wisconsin. There was a rock in the pit of my stomach when he left my house the morning of April 11. We held each other in my doorway and cried. We'd only be apart for three weeks, but we had both been so happy, high on whatever love hormone is produced and released to cause those great waves of bliss. I busted that bubble for us. My craving to stay aligned with the woman I had grown into prior to meeting him was as important to me as staying in our love bubble. It felt as though I was somehow betraying myself by not returning to Wisconsin, even if it was for a shortened time. In the end, loving myself won. But my heart sank a bit as I watched him walk out of my patio.

Before long, my mom came by to take me to the airport, and by the afternoon I was in Wisconsin and unpacking my things one more time.

Chapter Sixteen

LISTENING TO MY HEART

THIS TIME AROUND, I WAS IN WISCONSIN BY MYSELF. GAVIN was diving into his new job in the real estate industry, and I was putting all my energy into everything that wasn't our love bubble.

My soul longed for that place, those kindhearted, friendly people, and the energy I felt being there. Even covered in snow, the landscape of Wisconsin inspired me, and I didn't waste a single day there. If I wasn't at a networking breakfast, I was at one for lunch or dinner. I accepted a last-minute opportunity to lead a media-pitching workshop at a conference center a friend of mine owned. And during my creative, daydreaming time that was blocked out on my calendar, I curled up next to the fireplace and made myself a fire.

That April was unusually cold. It snowed most of the month, which I loved. My childhood closet had long wool sweaters and boots I'd worn during the winter of 2017, items that didn't have any place in Arizona. I let Wisconsin fuel me, overflow my creative tank, and move me. It wasn't as romantic or electric as the bubble I had been in with Gavin, but I loved it just the same.

Gavin and I had spent so much time together that being apart allowed me to process the numerous thoughts firing through my brain each hour—about him, us, and me being in a relationship as an entrepreneur, in a relationship with a dad, and how I could possibly balance it all.

As I started to share my new relationship with more friends and clients, everyone would say, "Speed kills. It's a good thing you have some space."

And then the next question was always, "So you're not moving back to Wisconsin?"

The fact was, I wanted to stay. My body felt better, lighter, more aligned with tall trees, green grass, creeks, ponds, rolling hills, and, most importantly, a seasonal change. The only reason I would stay in Arizona was for Gavin. And until I was ready to do that, I would respond to anyone who asked me about my living arrangements by saying, "Moving back full time has been postponed."

I had never before been in a position to throw out plans I made for my own life or in the name of love. I had never questioned if I could be that kind of woman or if my heart was that generous. I wanted to be her. I wanted to give that much. And still, I knew what happened to my spark, my spirit, when I gave it over completely to something. It was overshadowed, became duller and disconnected. Burnout had taught me that.

It was just over two weeks into my stint in Wisconsin when Gavin brought up my return ticket one night. "Are you looking forward to coming back home?" he asked.

The truth was, I was excited to see him but not necessarily about returning to the desert.

"Mostly just seeing you," I said.

"Well that's good," he laughed. He was happy I remembered what he looked like and wanted to see him again.

Our conversation that night looked at the reality of our situation. I was considering staying in a place I wanted to leave because of him. And my fear was that the weight of it would be too much for either one of us to bear. I voiced my concerns, and we talked out what we could see through and made promises that our communication would always be crystal clear. I could feel the love we had for another and the dedication we had to growing together two thousand miles away. It felt strong, healthy, and honorable.

I cried myself to sleep that night. Not out of pain or heartbreak but for feeling deeply, romantically loved for possibly the first time in my life. The wave of emotion was intense, and the pressure of that truth sat on my lower belly for a while. I held my belly and let myself cry. I honored myself, who I'd grown into, and who I wanted to grow into next.

When I woke the next day, the only emotion waiting for me to recognize it and tap into it was love. My heart raced, angel bumps covered my legs and arms, and shivers ran up my spine.

The last few days in Wisconsin crept by. I didn't worry about networking events or saying goodbye to friends. I completed whatever work I already had on my calendar and signed off as early as possible to practice deep self-love and self-care. I spent as much time outside as I could stand, even if it was still winter.

My walks around the pond were intentional and gentle. I'd sit on the bench to meditate just as I had the previous year. With each inhale, I'd picture rays of sun pouring into the top of my head and moving easily through my body, lighting up any dark or otherwise unreachable parts of my spirit and heart. With every exhale, I'd imagine thick tree roots inching their way from the base of my feet into the core of Earth. I was supported, safe, loved, healthy, and overflowing with wisdom and clarity.

The bench was frozen, and my butt went numb pretty quickly. Still, I'd sit there as long as I could hear, sense, know, or feel God talking to me. The same questions or topics came to mind during these chats and meditation sessions.

God, is Gavin the man I am meant to live my life with?

I'd feel pressure on my heart and took that as a *yes* from God.

How can I keep this feeling in my body when I return to the desert?

Tingles would run up my legs.

What more can I do in my business?

Nothing really came to mind, and I took that as a sign that I was supposed to stay focused on my personal life.

Normally I'd just throw all my clothes in my suitcase and be ready to leave for the airport in a few minutes. This time around, I packed little by little over the last few days. I placed my suitcase on a hope chest at the foot of the bed, and every time I passed it,

I put in a shirt, pair of jeans, panties, socks, bras, capri pants, or pajama set that I'd left there over the years of my healing. I didn't know when I would return. It could be in two months. It could be in a year. Everything was unknown and exciting.

There were two extreme feelings running through my body at any point throughout the last few remaining days there. It felt like the night before Christmas, and I was giddy beyond measure. And there was a sadness present, too. I understood them both and honored both. When I could feel the excitement for my return to the love bubble, I moved my body with a little dance party and big bursts of laughter. When the sadness for leaving, and possibly not returning, was there, I curled up in a chair and took deep breaths.

Two other factors messed with my emotions those last few days in Wisconsin: it was a full moon and I had my period. Both were heavy, exceptionally painful, and created big waves of release. Short bursts of energy, minute-long dance parties, and deep breaths were pretty much all I could muster up.

The full moon has always messed with my sleep patterns, so I wasn't surprised when insomnia kicked in. The pain in my lower abdomen, back, and pelvis, though, was something I hadn't experienced since my fertility treatment days. I typed my gynecologist's name into my phone and sent a text.

Hi, Susan! Long time! I've been avoiding messages and calls from the office. I'll schedule something soon. Having a really heavy, painful period.

Susan didn't respond until much later in the day. Her response reminded me to get on her schedule, take care of myself, and if my periods continued to be bad, we could discuss birth-control methods.

A raw wave of grief ripped through my body after reading her text. I melted even deeper into the chair and turned off my phone. No need to reply.

Finally, the morning to leave came. Since I hadn't fallen asleep the night before, I was able to wash, dry, and put away the towels and sheets I'd used. I lugged my suitcase down the stairs, turned off the hot water, and locked up the house. The car came to get me as the sun peeked over the treetops.

I checked my bag, bought a few snacks, and walked up and down the terminal hallways as long as possible to get out all my nervous energy. The excitement to see Gavin had overtaken the sadness. The pressure in my pelvis and pain in my back was still there, but mostly, I just wanted to get to Gavin.

I texted him once I was in my seat on the airplane.

*On the plane heading back! *Kissy face emoji.**

I'm looking forward to seeing you! Can I take you to dinner tonight?

I'd love that!

*See you soon. *Kissy lips emoji.**

I took my journal, a pen, cell phone, and earphones out of my purse and stuck them in the seat pocket in front of me. I kicked my purse underneath the chair, turned on some music, and stuffed the earphones into my ears. I said a prayer for the plane to get there safely. I said a prayer for the pilots to be the best at their jobs today. I said another prayer for the rest of the passengers to board faster and that the pain sitting on my tailbone and hip joints to be removed.

Every minute of the three-and-a-half-hour flight felt like thirty. I played a few rounds of solitaire on my phone, got on the airplane's Wi-Fi, watched a few episodes of one of Guy Fieri's shows on Food Network, and a few *Friends* reruns.

The butterflies and jitters running through my body prevented me from sleeping. With more than an hour to go still, I grabbed my journal and a pen from the seat pocket and tried to get my nerves out on paper.

The ground was getting closer. I hit the "settings" button on my phone and hovered my index finger over the airplane icon. The second the wheels touched down, I clicked the icon and sent Gavin a text.

*I'm in Arizona! *Kissy lips emoji.**

It took a bit for the text to go through.

My next text was to my parents.

I landed. Still taxiing. I checked a bag. Meet you outside at door 7.

Gavin's text came back first.

*Can't wait to see you. *Happy face guy emoji.**

I collected my things, got a thumbs-up from my mom, and raced to baggage claim as if my speed was equal to the airport employees'.

While waiting for my bag, I thought out all sorts of responses to Gavin's text.

Should I ask him if I can bring an overnight bag?

Should I be flirty, sexy, or fun?

What if he liked all the space he's had these last three weeks?

I didn't have a chance to write anything. My bag popped out before I could come up with the perfect reply, so I put my phone away. My mom was waiting for me when I walked out of the terminal, and we were on the road within seconds. I moaned slightly when I sat down in the passenger seat, the pain and pressure on my pelvis uncomfortable, but being in motion toward Gavin made my heart buzz. My mom asked about my trip, who I saw, my work, Gavin, and if I had dinner plans.

"Gavin and I are going out for dinner," I said.

"That's great!"

"I'll let you know about Sunday night plans. I don't want to make plans just yet."

"Yep, just let us know. I don't have anything special planned for dinner this weekend."

My mom dropped me off at home, and I unpacked everything in my suitcase right into the washing machine. I had a few hours before I'd see Gavin so I made use of my time with housework, checking the mail, paying whatever bills I had for the month, and sending out an e-blast to my followers.

I went with cute, flirty text messages to Gavin. I sent him a selfie of me blowing him a kiss. He sent a selfie of himself smiling. I sent a picture of my living room with the message, *It's nice to be home.*

We agreed that I would meet him at his house when he got home from work and play dinner by ear. I slipped into a dress I hadn't worn in years and packed an overnight bag just to be on the safe side. I locked up my house and threw my bag in the back. Gavin was home already when I pulled up.

Before I left, I didn't have to knock on the door or ring the doorbell. He had given me a garage door opener and I could let

myself in. This felt a bit different. It felt as though we were starting all over again. I went with the doorbell and fidgeted with my
dress while I waited, shifting my weight from hip to hip.

He opened with a big smile and outstretched arms. I laughed
and hopped up and down a bit before leaning into his hug. It was
so great to be with him. We held each other for a while, and the
kiss he gave me started out sweet and light and turned passionate.
He led me into the kitchen, where he had two cocktails already
made, sitting on the counter.

He handed me one.

"Cheers," I said.

"Welcome home," he said.

We took seats next to each other on the couch. I tucked my
feet underneath his thighs, my knees leaning against his chest,
and he had his arm wrapped around my back.

He sighed. "This is better," he said.

We didn't talk much. I snuggled into his neck, spilling a few
drops of my drink on his dress shirt.

"Oh shoot, I'm sorry," I said.

I started to get up to get a towel. He pulled me closer.

"I don't care," he said.

I kissed him and took several long drags from my martini. I
made a pretty decent dent in it and set it down on the ground
away from our feet. I curled back into him. We stayed like that
until he finished his drink.

There was so much chemistry there between us. I wondered
if he could feel it, too. We had rushed into a committed relationship, had spent three weeks apart, and now it felt like we were

suspended in an electricity bubble running wild with hormones, love chemicals, and lust. And yet, there was an awkwardness about us. My mind was racing.

What is he thinking about?

Should I ask him about dinner plans so we get out of the house?

I need to change my tampon.

That last thought struck me. I pushed myself out of our cuddle fest and pulled him off the couch with me. "Let's go out and get something to eat before we melt into this couch," I said.

That clearly gave him an idea. He fell backward onto the couch with me in his arms.

Eeny Meeny Miny Moe. Should I tell him I have my period?

I gave in to our make-out session for a while, then stopped it abruptly and laughed.

He moaned.

Eventually, we made it out of the house to one of his favorite bars. My heart was bursting with pure joy. I had the man I loved next to me. I had a pretty dress on. My hair looked cute. There was a dirty martini in front of me and a brand-new tampon in place.

Life doesn't get any better than this!

The next two months were a big blur. We fell right back into a rhythm that worked for us. During the weeks he had the kids, we'd call each other every day and text sweet messages a few times a day. During the weeks he didn't have his children, I'd pack a bag and stay at his house a few nights. He would stay at mine at least once a week. We traded off where we hung out over the weekends.

I had a key to his house. He had a key to mine. We'd cook together, fall asleep next to each other, and even found a TV series we wanted to watch together. I carved out my own schedule within our relationship to fuel my creativity, self-love, and self-care. I'd roll out of bed, make a cup of coffee, and do a quick video for my storytelling clients, which usually included a meditation. When Gavin got up for his morning workout, I'd take Princess Leia on a little hike into the mountains he lived near. Before he left for work, I'd make us a hot breakfast. We'd kiss goodbye and go about our days.

And then one afternoon in late June, he came home from work and something was different. I was at the top of the stairs when he walked in.

"Hello," he said.

"Hi, honey," I responded.

He put his things down on the counter and turned to walk upstairs. The tone of his voice wasn't different. His smile was. And I felt a pain in my heart when our eyes met.

I walked into the bedroom and sat down on the bed. "What's wrong?" I asked when he walked in.

He looked at me. "I don't think I can live with anyone just yet. I'm not ready."

Lightning wrenched open my heart and ripped open my lower abdomen. I clenched my hands in my lap and dug my fingernails into the palm of my heart. I took a few deep breaths. He stood across from me, and we stared at each other.

"I didn't think we were living together. We spend a lot of time together when you don't have your kids, though. You want to spend less time together?"

I curled my toes under and tightened every muscle in my legs and butt, and exhaled.

"I realized I have more healing to do before I can be in another committed relationship," he said.

I couldn't respond. I stood up, hoping I wouldn't fall apart in front of him. I gathered the things I had in his closet that I could easily see and walked out of his room, down the stairs, and out the front door without turning around.

Just get into the car and drive away.

Stop sign.

Turn right.

Don't hit the kids in the street.

Don't cry.

Get out of the neighborhood.

Green light.

Pull into this parking lot. It's far enough from his house. You can cry now.

I parked in a spot facing an empty baseball field. I turned on the radio and held my face in my hands as my heart broke and tears rushed out.

Chapter Seventeen

NOW WHAT?

I TOSSED MY OVERNIGHT BAG IN THE CORNER OF MY BEDROOM, threw decorative pillows on top of it, and crawled into bed. The pain in my body was so sharp it hurt to move. My body was practically convulsing from crying, and pain was all I felt. Waves of sobs came out, making it my breath catch in my rib cage. I couldn't exhale. I had to sit up, or even stand, to force air out.

Every trigger from my life that I hadn't yet healed about feeling unwanted, being a burden, unworthy, and unlovable was in front of me. Those triggers made the shame, embarrassment, and guilt run wild through my head.

I healed this already. I know I'm worthy of love. I am a loving, lovable woman. I take care of myself and work on myself all the time. I shouldn't feel ashamed.

Deep down I knew we had moved too fast, and I did blame myself for not listening to that faint voice in the back of my mind. And then I blamed him for not communicating his needs and fears and for misleading me that we were in a safe environment.

Mostly, though, I blamed myself.

I should have slowed us down. I should have made sure we had more space.

The reality was, I was deeply in love with a man I thought I'd marry one day. All the shoulda, coulda, wouldas were pointless. We were the perfect puzzle pieces for each other, and I craved that. I doubt I would have lived our relationship any differently if we'd had a do-over.

I left his house in the middle of the week, and gratefully I only had a few clients to work with that Thursday and Friday. I gave myself until Saturday to figure out what to say to him. I replayed every conversation about our relationship. I searched for red flags. The thing that I kept coming back to was the pace.

Speed kills.

Speed may have killed the relationship I was in, but space from it didn't just bust my love bubble. It gave me time to move from being sad, stunned, and ashamed to angry.

I didn't want to reach out to him in anger. I knew that wouldn't solve anything. We were two people who needed to do some healing work on ourselves in order for a relationship to actually work.

I didn't share the news about my relationship limbo with anyone. I wanted to make sure I correctly relayed what was happening, and since I wasn't sure yet, I stayed quiet. In fact, I barely spoke. If I didn't have a client call, I stayed still, introspective, and wrote. The more I journaled, the easier it was to take deep breaths.

Years before, when I would travel for Severson Sisters, I'd often be by myself. My mom and I came up with a code so she would know I was safe. If she texted me this code, I'd have to text it back or she'd call the cops.

I got the code from my mom a lot during those next few days. It was as if her motherly instinct kicked in. My heartbreak radar must have gone off like the Bat-Signal or something. My parents were already summering in Wisconsin so our Sunday dinners weren't happening. As much as I love my parents, I was grateful I had some space so I could avoid another conversation about my love life. I'd have to tell them eventually, but I could put it off for at least a week. I knew I needed to talk to Gavin to feel certain about where we were and if this was a *break* or a *breakup* before I shared anything.

The Saturday after I'd left Gavin's house arrived, and I had to text him. I figured the best way to reach out for the first time would be between thoughts, as if it were out of habit and I didn't have to feel or overthink anything. After my morning coffee, I went to my corner market. I pushed a cart through the doors and grabbed the first overpriced bouquet of flowers I saw.

Flowers will make me feel better.

I rolled right past all the healthy and good-for-me food and went right to the meat counter. I hadn't made myself a steak in years and asked for a T-bone. The butcher asked if I cared which one I got. I pretended that I knew what I was doing, or as if it really mattered, and took a second to pick it out. I pointed to the one closest to me, making him come out from behind the case and open it right in front of me.

I'll make tonight a date night. I can treat myself.

I also asked for a few Chicago-style hot dogs and prepared meatballs, and I picked up some wine, cheese, crackers, chips, chocolate, a two-pound container of red potato salad, a bag of bagels, and some cream cheese. I checked out and texted Gavin on the way to the car.

To be clear, did you break up with me?

I put my phone in my purse, placed my bags on the passenger seat, and drove home. I heard it chime as I pulled into my parking spot. I left the car running while I checked my phone.

I'm not ready for such an intense relationship yet.

I stared at the screen. An ache deep in my gut throbbed. There wasn't anything I could say that was friendly, loving, kind, or compassionate so I turned off my phone, grabbed my groceries, and walked as fast as I could into my house before the storm I could feel building up inside ripped me apart.

I can't believe I got this wrong.

Should I just continue on with my old plans now?

I can't breathe.

That day crept by, and all I wanted was for it to be over. I wanted a clean start. I put the flowers in a vase with the plastic wrap around them. At least I added water. I changed right back into my pajamas, slathered way too much cream cheese on a bagel, and smashed the top and bottom together. I picked at it as I searched my television for anything with John Candy in it. I pushed "play" on *The Great Outdoors*. I sat in the corner of my couch with a bag of chips and a chocolate bar next to me and watched movie after movie.

I fell asleep before I could make myself the steak or get to *Armed and Dangerous*. I did put a nice dent in the potato salad, had two Chicago-style hot dogs, and a good amount of chocolate.

Besides forcing myself to go to church on Sunday, the next day was pretty much the same except I traded out John Candy for Chevy Chase. I got through the rest of the potato salad, another bagel, and was about to make myself the steak when Gavin sent a text.

I do love you. I'm just not ready.

I took that as his way to end our relationship. My heart was shattered, and I didn't need to tell him that. The worst part about it was that I didn't believe we were finished. This didn't feel like two mismatched souls trying to make it work. It felt like a detour that wasn't on the damn map. And there wasn't anything I could do about it.

The first weekend was over with, and I was glad to dive into work come Monday. I stacked that week with clients and house-work. I practiced self-care by making sure I walked outside once a day and showered once a day. I made appointments to get my teeth cleaned and to have my annual visit to my gynecologist. In between, I nursed my shredded heart with better food and a new project—my fortieth birthday. It was still a month away but thinking about it gave me something to put my energy into.

Gavin was never really off my mind. He was always in the back-ground like an instrumental soundtrack. Some days he sounded above all the other noise running amok in my head, and other days I was able to keep all the other thoughts a bit louder than he was. It didn't make moving on from him any easier. I tried writing out my feelings in letters to him that I would then burn. I tried removing the dress shirt and other clothes he left at my house and putting them in a box under my bed so I wouldn't see them. Lastly, I decided to mail his key back to his house. I hadn't said much to him through text messages in weeks. We never spoke over the phone and hadn't seen each other in about a month. It was time. I ripped a piece of paper out of my journal and wrote:

Gavin,

Since we aren't in a relationship anymore, I don't want your key. You can send mine back now, too.

I really thought we were it. I saw a life together and am having a lot of trouble moving on. Not having a key to your place here might help.

Carrie

A few days later I got a text from him. He got the key, said he'd return mine, and apologized for hurting me. Enough time had gone by. I *thought* I was mature enough to have a clear conversation with him about the breakup.

I still can't see where we broke, I texted.

It was just too intense too soon. I just got divorced, he texted.

I thought about it. It always came back to the pace. I remembered conversations I would have with my girlfriends and even my mom and sister over the years.

When I was younger and thought about the man I would end up creating a life with, I always envisioned the same picture. I figured I'd meet someone, know him as a soul mate, and fall into a life together quickly.

When you know, you know.

My friends would always say, just be sure to date him for an entire year before you get married. My mom and sister always agreed with my vision. I dated a lot of men but never the same man for long. If he wasn't the person I wanted to create a life with after a month or so, I'd move on. I never wanted just any relationship. I wanted my partner in life. That's one of the reasons I had planned to move back to Wisconsin. I didn't think my partner was in Arizona. It felt like I had dated all the men out there already. Gavin had come out of left field like those baseball ghosts who asked Kevin Costner if his cornfield was Heaven. And now, maybe because Gavin needed time and space, I had to recreate the life I thought I had finally manifested.

The thought of being single again came crashing down on my gut. I had been doing that for forty years. I had been single just a few months ago. I knew how to do that. I could continue doing that. It hurt like hell, though, and I lacked my usual sparkle.

I can't help that we met so soon after your divorce. If you don't want me, I'll go forward with my plans to move back to Wisconsin, I texted.

A piece of me knew it was passive aggressive and a bigger piece of me hoped he'd ask me to stay.

I wish you all the very best, then, if that's what you decide to do.

The anger I had kept a tight lid on reached a boiling point in that moment. All sensibility left my brain, and my repressed inner wild bitch, who only came out when absolutely necessary, took over.

Move over, lady. I got this. Who is this guy and why haven't we laid into him yet?

My fingers flew over my phone as I texted. *You wish me well? What the fuck is that? You're really okay if we never see each other again?*

I knew it was dramatic. I could see him again. My parents have a home in town and so does my sister. I'd be back. *Shut up,* I told my rational brain. *I need to get this out.*

My phone dinged with another text from him. *You have to do what's best for you, and I have to do what's best for me.*

You're a coward. We lived a mile apart for nearly a decade. We worked across the street from each other for five fucking years. We went to the same bars on the same nights and never met. You had to get divorced for us to finally meet, and now you don't want this life we could have.

It's not that I don't want it, Carrie. It's that it's too much too soon.

Gavin was consistent. I just couldn't accept it or hear it. I was so ready for a lifelong partnership and blinded to anything he had to say.

I deleted his number. My inner wild bitch was also very child-like and inconsolable.

Chapter Eighteen

THE INNER VOICE

BY THE BEGINNING OF JULY, I HAD LEARNED THAT THE REAson my periods had been so painful for the last several months was because of a golf ball–sized fibroid in my uterus. My doctor told me that if I ever planned to conceive a child, the fibroid had to be surgically removed with a procedure called a myomectomy. And the sooner the better.

Even though I wasn't in a relationship, I still wanted the possibility of conceiving so I booked the procedure for later that month. I wanted to get through my birthday party and turning forty without my uterus being the main focal point *again*.

My parents and an uncle came to town to celebrate with me. We planned a great few days together. We saw an off-Broadway production of *Mary Poppins*, one of my favorites. My uncle, sister, and I found an open roller rink. And another afternoon we drifted along in a lazy river on inner tubes. It was perfect, and I felt totally loved.

It was easier to breathe, the crying had subsided, and Gavin was on my heart more than my mind. I leaned into the pain I felt and used it to reshape what I wanted.

A new voice and version of my identity had started to emerge from the deepest part of me. This new Carrie was the most unapologetic.

I wanted a partner who saw all pieces of me, from the inner wild bitch to the spiritual side. I wanted a career I adored, filled with opportunities to support women who were also unleashing their unapologetic voices. I wanted a family. Mostly, I wanted to be seen, heard, and witnessed.

By the time I turned forty, I knew I was ready to move back to Wisconsin. My plan was to get through the fibroid surgery and pack up my life to head back to Wisconsin when I felt strong enough to do so. I figured I would be back in time for the winter months. I was told that I would be very weak and sore after the surgery and wouldn't be able to lift anything heavy for a while, so I didn't buy a ticket back to Wisconsin but decided that it was best I leave and continue on with my plans pre-Gavin.

My mom stayed in town after my fortieth birthday to help me through the surgery. It had felt like decades since my IVF days and the last time someone had to help me through a situation that would allow me to possibly have a child.

After the paperwork and signing all the liability forms, I was taken back to pre-op. The doctor came in and explained the myomectomy. She would try to remove the fibroid first by going up through my lady parts. If she couldn't reach it that way, she would have to make an incision in my abdomen to access the uterus. She'd make a slit on my bikini line, take out my uterus to clean it up, and put everything back together again. If she needed to do an abdominal myomectomy, I'd be in the hospital for two nights.

Great.

A nurse came in, shot me up with drugs, and in no time at all everything went foggy.

As soon as I opened my eyes, Gavin's face flashed through my mind, and I heard that inner voice shout loud and clear, *Call Gavin!*

Even in my drugged-up haze, I was surprised. In the past, that voice was always my inner guidance system. I listened to her. Or it. Or God. Whatever it was, I trusted it. And this time, I knew I'd heard it right. *Call Gavin.* I saw his face and couldn't blink his damn blue eyes out of the way. My body was weightless and I was high on whatever drugs the hospital had me on, but I was awake and I'd gotten a clear message. Gavin was the last person I wanted to think about right there and then. I just had something removed from the deepest, most feminine part of my body. I wanted to think about the future, not the past. So I pretended it hadn't happened.

My mom was standing over me, smiling. She grabbed my hand and stroked my hair.

"Did she get it?" I asked her.

"Yes, she did," my mom said.

The doctor came in just then to explain the golf ball wasn't cancerous. I looked at my mom, and she pursed her lips. I guess I'd forgotten to tell my mom that there had been a slight possibility that the fibroid would be cancerous and, in that event, inoperable. The doctor went on to say she'd had to cut me open to remove the fibroid and I would need to stay in the hospital longer than anticipated.

"But it's okay now? It's clean?" I asked.

"It's perfect," the doctor said. She squeezed my feet and left.

After some time, I was rolled upstairs into my own room and had a new set of nurses caring for me. The first one came in to get my vitals and recorded them on a whiteboard. She put socks with sticky bottoms on my feet and laid another blanket across my legs. She went over some guidelines and suggestions for my stay. I agreed not to get up without help. If I had to use the restroom, I needed to call a nurse. If the painkillers wore off, I could ring for a nurse and one would administer something. I needed to eat, and later that day, I would need to walk up and down the hallway. Walking was my job when I wasn't sleeping or too groggy.

The pain was pretty severe at first, even with the drugs. I followed the guidelines and slept when I could. And during the moments I was alone in the hospital room, I thought back to that inner voice.

Call Gavin.

He had no idea where I was or what I was going through. At least, I didn't think he did. It had been a little over a month since we'd last communicated. I wondered if I could remember his number.

Something, something, something, something, something, something, something, something, something, something.

Nope. I'd try again later, and maybe it would come to me.

Walking hurt and gave me the sweats. Sitting down back in bed hurt, too. Big purple bruises formed along my abdomen, and I looked very pregnant. Everything was swollen, and nothing felt right on or in my body.

Two days later, I was discharged with prescriptions for two weeks' worth of a heavy-duty painkiller and an extra-large dose of an anti-inflammatory that I could take at various times. It was recommended that I not drive or do much exercise for the next month. My mom offered a spare bedroom in her house for me to recoup in, and I was so grateful. It was still summertime in Phoenix, and she had never spent the summer there before.

For the first week, I said yes to both the painkiller and the anti-inflammatory whenever time allowed, and I slept a lot. The pain was constant. We used the hospital's pain rating system. Most of the time, I was between a five and seven. There were days I was weepy, and on those days, I cradled my body and gave myself a lot of grace.

He was still the face I saw when I opened my eyes. And the words *Call Gavin* played on repeat in my mind. One night I tried to remember his number again. The area code flashed in my mind along with the last four digits.

If I think of the first three, I'll send a text.

My mom and I watched reruns of old shows, she brought me soup in bed, and I listened to her whenever she told me it was time to get up and go for a walk. I tried to be a good patient.

We walked a little longer each day. At first, it was just up and down hallways for a few minutes several times a day. Then we walked up and down the driveway two or three times a day. We added the street on next and then the block. We were slow and gentle. I took fewer and fewer pills the second week to ensure I didn't become dependent upon them, so by the time she left to go back to Wisconsin a few weeks after my surgery, I wasn't taking painkillers and could drive myself around.

The pain was barely there when I said goodbye to my mom, but I was still swollen with a bulging, purple scar across my bikini line. I wasn't walking much faster, and nothing in my closet felt good on my body. My sister had bought me a dress a few sizes too big that I could pull over my head, and I wore that to the grocery store whenever I needed to go. Besides that, I lived in robes and nightshirts.

One night when I was lying in bed, the first three digits of Gavin's number came to mind. I said his full number out loud. I knew it was right.

I really don't want to text him. He broke my heart. Putting myself out there again is stupid.

I heard the same phrase again. *Call Gavin.*

What for? What should I say to him?

Just let him know you're still in town.

Fine.

I picked up my phone, opened up the message icon, and punched in his number.

Hi, Gavin. This is Carrie. I hope you're doing well. I thought you would want to know I just had surgery here in town. I'm fine. The last we communicated I said I was leaving, but as it turns out, that's not the case. I do hope you're doing good. Take care.

I hit "send." *There. I did it.*

My phone was still in my hand when it rang.

"Hello?" I answered.

"Hi," Gavin said.

"Hi," I said.

"What was your surgery for?"

"I had to have a fibroid removed."

"From what?"

Pause.

"My uterus."

Pause.

"But you're okay?"

"I'm okay. I move really slowly right now and can't do anything but light walking. I look puffy everywhere, but yeah, I'm okay. How are you?"

"Miserable."

My breath was stuck in my body, and tears pooled in my eyes.

"I made a big mistake, Carrie."

I didn't know what to say.

"Can I see you?"

That moment felt hopeful and painful in the same breath. I wanted to see him and wanted to protect my heart at the same time. I glanced down at my swollen body. I looked different from the last time he saw me, and a touch of insecurity rushed through my entire being.

"Why don't you stop by tomorrow night?" I suggested.

"Great. I'll stop by after work."

"Sounds good. Have a good night."

"You too."

I sure hadn't been expecting *that*.

My heart was zinging through every part of my body. I put my phone down and stared at it for a minute. A smiled pulled at the corners of my lips, and a little laugh escaped. I went to bed that night feeling excited about the next day for the first time in a while.

The following morning was slow and calm. I did my morning walk before the August heat became too much to bear. I meditated and journaled about my body and how much I appreciated all it's been through. I did my client calls from my desk and all other work from the couch.

By four o'clock, I stopped working for the day and took my time getting ready for Gavin's visit. I tried on a few different pairs of yoga pants since anything with a button was out of the question. Even form-fitting yoga pants made me want to scream. My belly had a mind of its own, and I just had to accept that it would be a different shape for a while. My options for the night weren't anything surprising. I could either wear my robe, my super baggy dress, or pajamas. I put on a clean pair of pj's and curled back up on the couch.

I got a text from Gavin right around the time he normally wrapped up work. He was on his way. When his headlights appeared in my family room window, my heart fluttered. I opened up the patio door and waited for him. Our eyes met when he rounded the corner, and we both smiled. I was squealing inside but kept my cool.

"Hi, Carrie," he said.

He hugged me as he stepped inside. He gave me a kiss on the cheek and watched me as I closed the door.

"It's nice to see you," I said.

We took a seat on the couch, him in one corner and me in the other. He wanted to know all about the surgery and my recovery process. We discussed his work, my work, my fortieth birthday, his kids, my family, and then finally, we were out of things to talk about. I stopped asking him questions. The silence in the room was refreshing.

Ask him what the deal is here. I don't think he's going to start this.

"So why are you miserable?" I started.

"I miss you," he said.

I let him talk.

"It was too much too fast, and I didn't expect to be in a serious relationship so soon. You're amazing, and I thought I needed to do the thing where I date women before settling down again."

My mind homed in on one piece of what he had just said.

"You've been dating other women, then?"

"Yes. I've gone out for drinks with three women. Nobody even came close to you or what we had."

That got a smile.

"I was on a date last night. We weren't a fit at all. When I drove home, I said a prayer and asked God for help in my love life, and literally, as I was praying, you sent me a text."

"Would you have reached out to me if I hadn't sent a text?"

He shook his head and shrugged his shoulders.

"You were really angry with me. I didn't think you wanted to hear from me again."

I told Gavin about the annoying, repetitive message I got in the hospital, two weeks before I'd gotten in touch with him.

"I'm glad you did. Can I see you again soon?"

Before he left, I suggested we start over and go slow.

"Let's start with a movie," I said.

I walked him to the door. He gave me a gentle kiss on the cheek again and said good night.

I need to remember to listen to that inner voice.

A movie turned into another date over drinks, and that turned into many dates over dinner. But we did take it slow for the first couple of months. I needed that. It allowed me the time and space to trust myself and trust that I could do the right thing for me and for our relationship. The love bubble was around us again, firmly in place, just in a different shape. Some days it had sharp edges, and other times it was a big, gushy heart.

Once we were back in sync, I made a commitment to myself to let him see all my pieces. He got to meet that inner wild bitch up close and personal, and the super hippy flower child who meditated on a rock next to a creek.

I spoke up when I needed space, time alone, time with him, a road trip, a date night, nothing more than a good friend to lean on, and so did he.

By the holidays that year, I had met his kids and his parents. Come spring of 2019, we discussed marriage, kids of our own, the type of home we would want to live in, and the careers we hoped to have. And when I started a new publishing business in the middle of 2019, Gavin was my biggest cheerleader.

I would write appreciation letters to God thanking Him for my dreams coming true, even if they hadn't yet. I'd sit in meditation and imagine how it would feel when I met a goal, and I allowed that feeling to flow through my entire body.

Manifesting Gavin and our relationship was something that showed up in my gratitude journal all the time. Tapping into the feeling of being loved and supported was never hard. I always knew how much he loved me. What always brought me to my knees in a big sobbing mess was when I would question my enoughness. That insecurity was triggered without warning, and if I didn't address it right in that moment, it simmered. Within a few days, it would boil over and everything in my life would become a mess. These triggers came from within my relationship but also from my business.

When Gavin and I were off, it was because one or both of us had healing to do. When I didn't feel confident talking to a new prospective client, it was because I forgot to turn on my inner light. During the days I questioned myself, independently or within my relationship, I poured as much as I could into my journal to gain clarity and relief.

Running a new business, while also deepening my relationship with Gavin, provided plenty of reminders that I can sometimes forget to love myself as much as I love everyone else and that there is a path to burnout and I know what happens when I cross it.

Despite the bumps in my road with Gavin and the wounds that cut me deeply, we always found our way together within a day, if not hours. It was always clear that we were two people making a conscious decision to do life together. It was us. As friends, as partners, and as lovers.

In the fall of 2019, signs of burnout started to show again. I was worn-out and working all the time. It happens when new businesses pop, and mine did. On a Sunday in September, I told him I thought I needed a road trip. Without thinking twice or questioning it, we took the first week off we could and hit the road. We roamed from town to town on back roads through Arizona with Princess Leia in the back. We stopped at little shops for local goodies and did as much hiking as we could. There wasn't a plan or real timeline. We gave ourselves a week to put our phones away and focus our energy on ourselves and on our love for each other.

We agreed to head back to Phoenix on a Friday. It was September 13, 2019. I woke up with a pressure on my heart. This vision kept coming to mind of Gavin and me walking hand in hand in a little town square that felt familiar but that we hadn't been to as a couple before.

"I want to take our time driving back today," I said.

"Sure. We just have to be back by tonight to welcome the boys home for the week," Gavin said.

"I think I'd like to stop in Flagstaff for lunch," I told Gavin as we packed up our things.

"Sounds good," he said.

As we got on the road that morning, we said a prayer and thanked God for our beautiful adventure. Gavin always thanked God for bringing me back into his life. I always thanked God for Gavin and for helping me personally grow into the woman

I had become. After that, we drove in silence for a few hours. I'd look over at Gavin, and the love chemical would just ooze out and tears would pool in my eyes. I'd blink them back and smile at him. It could have been the full moon happening that night, or it could have been the fact that I was at peace, sitting next to the man I'd manifested, with the windows down and the crisp fall air of northern Arizona making my skin tingle.

We pulled into Flagstaff around lunchtime and found a parking spot on a side street. We took Princess Leia for a walk, let her run around a park for a while, and loaded her back in the car with the rear windows rolled down. Gavin grabbed my hand and led me around town, pointing out stores he thought I would like. We got to a shop that had crystals and wind chimes in the window.

"This place totally looks like you," he said.

I laughed and inhaled deeply. The smell of essential oils and sage was pretty inviting. Gavin followed me inside. The shop was small and filled with jewelry, books, clothing, oils, crystals, candles, and so much more. I did love stores like that. I didn't need anything or notice anything that caught my eye, though. As I turned to walk out, I got another little tug deep inside. My attention was being called over to a small case in the corner of the shop. I looked down into it and saw one-of-a-kind rings made with all kinds of different crystals, stones, and gems. Purple stones, green stones, blue stones, and one gold. A store employee and Gavin both walked over to the case to join me.

"What calls to you?" Gavin asked.

All the rings were beautiful, but the gold stone in the upper right corner of the case made the hair on my arms stand up. I had never seen anything like it. I pointed to it and looked at the employee. She unlocked the case and placed the ring box on the counter.

"Try it on," Gavin said.

I slid it on the ring finger of my right hand and held my hand out in front of me.

"I love it," I said.

"It's made with a gold quartz," the employee said.

A little card was pressed into the lid of the box. Gavin read it aloud.

"*The Golden Healer Quartz represents spiritual communication, energy enhancement, restores your body's balance, and brings joy, peace, and harmony.* That sounds just like you."

I smiled at him and laughed softly.

"Try it on the other hand," Gavin said.

My whole body buzzed with excitement. If my body could have burst sparkles and glitter in that moment, it would have. I slid it on the ring finger of my left hand and instantly felt a surge of bliss, anticipation, and love rush up and down my body. I held my hand out in front of me and wiggled my ring finger back and forth for a few seconds. It looked like me. It was different, eclectic, one-of-a-kind, and sharp around the edges. I glanced over at Gavin with tears in my eyes, giggling.

Gavin and the employee gave me some time to get the overflow of emotion out of my system. I left it on my hand and wiggled my finger around.

"We'll take this one, please," Gavin said.

I handed the ring to the employee and looked at Gavin. We stood in place, staring at each other and smiling. He grabbed my hands, and I expected him to drop to his knee right there in the corner of a crystal shop. Instead, he stepped closer, kissed me gently, and held me, heart to heart.

We didn't say anything. I knew what was happening. We had discussed getting engaged before. He had my parents' blessing already. He always said he wanted to find the perfect ring before he asked me.

He let me go and walked over to the register where the employee was waiting, watching us patiently.

I walked to the door and took a few deep breaths while he paid and the employee bagged it up for him. He took my hand again once we got back on the sidewalk and led me down the street to a sushi restaurant a block away.

"Let's try this place for lunch," he said.

"Sounds good."

Just be cool, Carrie. Just because he bought a ring doesn't mean this is happening today.

We both ordered a lunch special and sat in silence. Smiling. Staring at each other. It was peaceful, romantic despite the fish smell and plastic dishware. The paper bag with my ring in it was next to Gavin on his bench. Our lunch came, and we took our time eating. He paid, and we were back in the car heading home.

There are two main roads we could have taken to get from Flagstaff to Phoenix. Gavin preferred to take the more scenic route through Sedona and Oak Creek Canyon. The road followed the creek, and the trees towered over us. It was much more beautiful than a main highway. Plus, we both loved the water. It wasn't unusual for Gavin to pull over on the side of the road for a little side adventure of investigating a creek, stream, or river.

"I'm going to stop at one of these scenic pull-outs along the road," Gavin said.

"Good idea," I said.

He passed a few spots that were already filled and slowed down at the next one he saw.

"Give me a minute. Let me see if it's worth going down there," he said.

The traffic was light. Gavin got out and found an easy trail down to the creek. I could see him from the car window. There wasn't anyone else down there but him. He turned around and waved at me to join me. I turned off the car and followed the path down to the creek. I expected Gavin to start skipping rocks, and I looked for a spot I could take my shoes off so I could feel the water on my feet. I heard cars above us. The creek was inviting, and the chirping birds brought me a deep sense of peace. It was a perfect setting. When I turned around, Gavin was on one knee with the ring box open in his hands.

I squealed, laughed, and cried all at the same time. We got engaged next to the creek in an organic, spontaneous, beautiful moment that was all ours. We spent some time playing in the water, took pictures, and got back in the car to keep on driving. Our love bubble was infused with a little more magic after that.

We smiled at each other and held hands in silence. Gavin glanced down at my ring, brought my hand up to his lips, and kissed it. My mind was spinning and totally blank. I couldn't catch a single thought.

We're engaged. We woke that morning boyfriend and girlfriend. What do people do now?

A few miles down the road, Gavin pulled into a bakery parking lot. We ordered a few desserts and called our parents to share the news.

I called my mom at home in Wisconsin first, then my dad at work, and texted my sister and brother a picture of Gavin and me next to Oak Creek after he proposed.

Gavin and I are engaged, I texted.

Congrats!!!! Holly wrote back.

That's great, my brother wrote.

Gavin called both his parents, too. Everyone was thrilled for us. And once that was through, we were back on the road heading home.

Even though we were the same people coming home as when we'd left, I felt different. My skin tingled. I felt energy running up and down my body. There was a fullness and tenderness within the depth of my heart I hadn't experienced before.

By the time Gavin pulled into his driveway, I was ready for some alone time.

Gavin took our bags inside his house, and I grabbed Princess Leia and headed out for a quick walk around the neighborhood before the sun completely set.

I turned a corner to wander up a trail away from all the houses and up into the mountain. I didn't want to be around people for a few minutes. I wanted some time to process our road trip, our engagement, and the overwhelming emotions swelling up inside me. I needed to let out a scream or a cry or both.

I walked as fast as I could and got to the top of the trailhead pretty quickly. I exhaled.

Inhale deep.

Exhale deeper.

Inhale.

Exhale.

I had so much energy. To shake some of it off, I busted out a dance party with Princess Leia, screaming, laughing, and crying.

Engagement didn't make me a different woman. It was just one more version of myself I had yet to explore. I could feel the start of another soul quest rushing in. Growth, exploration, expansion, and new levels of self-love waited for me.

And it started all over again.

Afterword

EVEN THOUGH THE ULTIMATE DREAM FOR MY LIFE ALWAYS included a partner and children, I understand that's not the vision every woman has for her life. And it's certainly not the road every woman has to take to love herself and see herself as unapologetically enough. I'm choosing to end this part of my story here because what happened next will fill an entire book.

Our engagement high lasted for the next handful of months. We scheduled our wedding for April 19, 2020, but the executive order to cancel all events over fifty people due to COVID-19 came down thirty-two days before our wedding.

We ended up postponing our wedding four times, had a small ceremony in September 2020 in the woods and a much smaller reception than originally planned in 2021.

This journey hasn't been an easy one. There's no fairytale here. As my dad would say, there have been many twists, turns, and just as many pit stops. Even when I was totally lost, I somehow found my way back home—to myself. It all served a greater purpose.

This self-discovery cracked me open and introduced me to a confidence and depth within myself I never knew I was missing. Stepping into my own light each day has been the biggest lesson I've learned as I reshaped what success and self-love mean to me.

I *am* unapologetically enough, just as I am.

And so are you.

Appendix A

EXERCISES TO REDEFINE SUCCESS

At the start of each year, I set an intention. The intention is typically summed up in a word or phrase. My intention for 2014, for example, was personal happiness. Not just happiness but *personal* happiness. It's my favorite feeling of them all!

Everyone's definition and understanding of happiness is different. I know people who are happy running full speed ahead without any free time in sight. I know people who are happy only on vacation. And I know people who operate from a permanent place of happiness.

I'm pretty sure I've been all those people at some point in my lifetime, and over the years my personal mission was to move back into a permanent place of happiness.

After I experienced my professional burnout in 2013, I realized that I welcomed a deeper level of happiness—both personal and professional. I was able to see that in order to move through my professional life happily, I first had to move through my overall life happily. And I've worked on myself enough to know that in order to bring about personal happiness, I first had to understand the feeling of happiness at a deeper level.

When I think of the feeling of happiness, I laugh. I laugh to the point of crying because I can feel it so deeply. I twirl and clap and dance when I think of what happiness feels like.

Throughout 2014, I focused on *activities* I knew would make me *feel* happy on a personal level. I trusted that when I moved from a place of personal happiness, everything I did professionally would mirror my personal life.

My 2014 personal-happiness action-item list looked like this:

1. Dance parties in the living room.
2. Write again.
3. Read more funny books.
4. Go on more road trips.
5. Cuddle more animals.
6. Take bike rides at sunset.
7. Play in the ocean.
8. Communicate more affectionately with loved ones.
9. Say yes to fun more often and invite friends to join in.

10. Wear fairy wings.
11. Make new friends.
12. Watch the clouds while lying in the grass.
13. Meditate to pretty music.

Playing in the ocean was really healing for me, which helped me open up my heart.

When I said yes to invites, new friends came into my life.

New friends gave me more reasons to communicate with loved ones!

My private dance parties, bike rides, fairy wings, and cuddle sessions with animals were really freeing for me, too.

More free moments helped me slow down to watch the clouds, write again, and meditate. And writing again gave me the creative outlet to give without attachment.

The best and probably most important result that came from my personal-happiness list was learning how to fully accept and trust in my journey. When I was able to embody that, I was able to see that my entire year had been one happy moment after another. It was honestly a year of light, and even when I was experiencing heartache or disappointment, I could still accept the light within me and around me.

We all go through our own lessons at the time we're fully able to understand and receive them.

In this section, I invite you to identify how it feels when you are living your most fulfilling life.

When do you feel most alive?

Redefining success was deeply connected to the feeling of happiness and doing things that made me happy.

Redefining Success Exercise One

CREATING SUCCESS ON YOUR NEW TERMS

W HEN I WENT BACK TO WORK AFTER MY BURNOUT RECOV-
ery and designed new boundaries for myself, I had to create
a new set of definitions for what success meant to me. It had to
look different in order for my story to unfold differently.

The definition of success that led me to burnout was related to
money and love. I chased money for my nonprofit. I fought for it.
I was in the trenches with thousands of other nonprofit leaders
killing myself for pennies. And if I won one, I was successful. The
problem was, I had to prove myself and the organization every
day in order to gain funds. It was toxic. And no matter how much

money I gathered, I never felt successful because I couldn't ever take my armor off. There was always tomorrow, and the game started all over again. I was always fighting and never satisfied.

Success = Money. It was my old way of being. It was my old way of thinking. It led to loneliness, depression, anger, depletion, fatigue, weight gain, sleepless nights, and burnout.

To gain and get something new, I had to do and be something new. So I sat down and thought of all the feelings I really wanted to associate with success.

I wanted success to make me feel happy, peaceful, free, soulful, alive, playful, and abundant—not in a money sense, in a *being* sense. From then on, my definition of success was associated with those seven words.

The next question I asked myself was *when* did I feel happy, peaceful, free, soulful, alive, playful, and abundant? This took a bit longer to answer and required some free-form writing and meditation.

I feel happiest when I'm connected to a loved one.

I feel peaceful after I meditate or partake in some self-care.

I feel free when I'm communicating my truth somehow.

I feel soulful when I'm writing or helping someone share their stories.

I feel alive when I'm taking action toward my dreams.

I feel playful when I dance.

I feel abundant when I'm at the line of my comfort zone and moving toward my dreams with ease.

After writing out these new definitions around success, I made sure to keep them in front of me. I took a picture of them and saved them to my phone as my screen saver. I sent them to my friends. I taped them to my mirrors and refrigerator.

It worked for me. I hope it helps you, too.

STEP 1: DEFINE SUCCESS

In the space below, write your own definition of success.

_____

_____

_____

_____

_____

STEP 2: HOW YOU WANT TO FEEL ABOUT SUCCESS

What emotions do you want to associate with success? Try to come up with five to ten emotions.

1. _____

2. _____

3. _____

4. _____

5. _____

6. _____

7. _____

8. _____

9. _____

10. _____

STEP 3: WAYS TO FEEL THE WAY YOU WANT

Write out some ways in which you can evoke those emotions.

_____

_____

_____

_____

_____

Redefining Success Exercise Two

SELF-EXAMS CAN HELP US GROW

USUALLY WE ONLY CLAIM THE PARTS OF OURSELVES THAT WE like, or that other people point out as positive attributes. Accepting the parts of myself that I wasn't proud of actually helped me expand. Maybe you are a controlling or jealous person and don't want to admit it. Get honest with yourself here. Nobody's looking.

STEP 1: HOW ARE YOU SHOWING UP?

Circle the words that represent how you see yourself.

Aggressive	Honorable
Ambitious	Independent
Angry	Jealous
Authentic	Joyful
Bad listener	Leader
Bossy	Loving
Bully	Loyal
Calm	Manipulative
Confident	Motivated
Controlling	Mature
Creative	Optimistic
Demanding	Patient
Determined	Persistent
Dishonest	Playful
Disrespectful	Rude
Empowered	Rule-breaking
Energetic	Sarcastic
Enthusiastic	Sassy
Excluding	Self-aware
Fearless	Selfish
Forgiving	Spiritual
Friendly	Steady
Funny	Strong
Gossip	Successful
Graceful	Supportive
Grateful	Thoughtful
Healthy	Threatening
Helpful	Tranquil

Trusting   Wise
Unique   Wonderful
Valuable

STEP 2: CHANGE YOUR VIEW

In the space below, list any word that you no longer wish to claim as your own. Use this as a time to identify anything you see in yourself that you wish to change. Write down why you want to change these things, as well.

_____

_____

_____

_____

_____

Redefining Success Exercise Three

WHAT DOES YOUR HEART DESIRE?

T O CREATE A CLEAR PATH TO SUCCESS, YOU FIRST HAVE TO know the direction in which you want your path to go. What do you *really* welcome? Who do you want to become? To help you get a clear picture of your heart's desires and where you want to go in the next year, my first recommendation is for you to write out a yearly living vision.

Grab a notebook or your computer and sit down somewhere quiet. Break down your life into parts you want to focus on this year. I typically write down a maximum of four areas each year—Family, Career, Home, and Health, for example.

Once you pick the areas in your life, write down how each area of life would look and feel in a perfect world. The *feeling* piece of this exercise is key. Keep your yearly vision somewhere close by, like in a nightstand or drawer in your office, and look at it at the start of each week or month.

For example, my 2021 yearly vision is below:

HOME

I walk through the door of our beautiful ranch-style house. As I enter, I feel at peace and know I am home. This place fills my heart. It matches the warmth and love I feel inside.

I look around our home and see bright tones, big bay windows, and comfortable furniture I can sink into. It's safe, inviting, and pretty. I smell fresh flowers and hear the wind chimes hanging in the trees outside. I move into a family room with a redbrick fireplace. My family is sitting there playing a game and laughing. Our dining room table is in the far corner. It's set for entertaining guests, with tall candles and fresh flowers. Modern chandeliers light up the house. Photographs of my husband, our children, and our extended families cover the walls.

I move into my dream kitchen, which has a place for everything we need. The long, white cabinets and walk-in pantry keep us organized and clutter free.

I look out our sliding glass doors to see the trees and the beautiful, lush garden my husband planted.

Our four bedrooms and home office give us just the right amount of space.

I feel deep gratitude for our wonderful sanctuary.

We found this perfect house in a family-oriented neighborhood. We love the community. It's close to a creek, park, walking trail, and schools. We easily afford the bills to grow together as a family.

FAMILY

My family lives in harmony. We communicate with ease, and my heart overflows with gratitude for my husband, best friend, and bonus kids. My heart flutters when my husband looks at me. He makes me laugh. He is gentle when he holds me, and his kiss melts away all my worries. We have the same values and life purpose of service. He is financially stable and abundant in all ways. He is a strong and reliable partner. Bills are paid off on time, and we work together to create a retirement plan that allows us to travel, provide for our children, and pass on greatness to our grandchildren.

We naturally work together as a unit and recognize the importance of each other in the life we create together. He encourages me when I am down and allows me to do the same for him. He surprises me with small to large tokens of love, from flowers to trips to Ireland.

We have a balance of give-and-take, and when the balance is off, we easily adjust. We work together daily in an open, honest, and loving manner. We have great adventures together that run the gamut of simply cooking dinner to traveling the world.

We raise our children with a solid moral understanding of love, peace, faith, and abundance. We have the same parenting method when it comes to discipline, and we share responsibilities as equals. He is as involved in the raising of our children as I am. He is a loving, understanding, and sturdy parenting partner.

CAREER

My career as a hybrid book publisher feels expansive. It matches my internal growth and confidence. As I evolve as a woman, so does the Unapologetic Voice House. I am proud to serve as CEO of the Unapologetic Voice House.

Soul clients continue to sign with us, and I feel so lucky to be the captain of this great ship. I am at peace with the unknown of where the Unapologetic Voice House is going and am rooted in faith that God guides me clearly on this path.

Unapologetically Enough creates a new market for me as an author, and I am excited as massive media and partnership opportunities come in to share the message. This is fun! And I take care of myself as I grow as an international best-selling author.

HEALTH

My body adjusts nicely to getting back into the rhythm of regular workouts after the pandemic. I find a studio that fits my budget and love moving my body. My daily walks fill up my cup and rejuvenate my spirit. I love fueling my body with healthy foods.

Weight I have been holding on to as a protective shield these last few years falls off easily, and my body and I are at peace. My mindset is a top priority, and I recognize when I need to spend more time on it. My breaks throughout the day are mental health check-ins that I look forward to. And I take naps whenever I want.

Redefining Success Exercise Four

SEE IT EVERY DAY

M Y NEXT RECOMMENDATION TO CREATE A CLEAR PATH TO success is to add a visual element to your yearly vision and make a vision board. This one will take a bit of time.

To create a vision board, you'll need a large piece of construction paper or poster board and some of your favorite magazines. The first step is to write down overall themes you notice in your yearly vision document. What comes up the most? Are you looking for love? A healthier lifestyle? To gain or give away more money? Write down all the themes you can find. Your vision board will be filled with images related to your yearly vision themes.

Words are my superpower so the yearly vision document helps me know where I'm going from a big-picture perspective.

Creating a vision board helps me know in what direction to step each day to gain my heart's desires.

Be as creative as you want. Glue images to your construction paper and put your vision board somewhere private where only you can see it. Look at this masterpiece of yours every single day before you leave your house, and let these images overflow your cup and set your day up right.

Redefining Success Exercise Five

SOUL CONTRACTS

AFTER MY BURNOUT EXPERIENCE, I STARTED TO LOOK AT myself as the CEO of my own life. I was in charge of my actions and my emotions. I was in charge of every step I took. And I could co-create with the Big U to live out something new. One morning I decided to break my life into different sections. I had been doing it for years with my yearly vision and vision board. I knew how to co-create with the Universe as a CEO and felt pretty comfortable with it.

I wondered what would happen, though, if I allowed different energy in my life to be in charge of different areas of my life. So on a piece of paper I wrote five words—*LOVE, HEALTH, MONEY, CAREER, MINDSET*. Next to each word I assigned roles:

LOVE = Chief Heart Officer
HEALTH = Chief Well-Being Officer
MONEY = Chief Financial Officer
MINDSET = Chief Operating Officer
CAREER = Chief Story Officer

Going a step further, I created ninety-day contracts for each position. I, as the CEO, was writing up a contract for my Chief Heart Officer, Chief Operating Officer, Chief Financial Officer, Chief Story Officer, and Chief Well-Being Officer.

In ninety days, as the CEO and each of the other positions, I agreed on certain goals and milestones to reach in those five areas of my life.

For me, meditation was key for these exercises. For twenty minutes at a time, I would sit in my chair and daydream about what my perfect life would look like in these five areas.

My love life was filled with harmony, romance, my soul mate, and our children. We had dogs running all over the place, and we went on outings and traveled. We were happy and filled with excitement. We had friends and family over for Sunday brunches and picnics in the backyard. We had date nights planned weekly and knew how lucky we were to have finally found each other.

My financial life was fluid. We had money coming in to pay for adventures to new cities, really good food, our house, and a strong self-care routine. We gave money to charities we believed in, and it felt so good. Abundance filled our lives, and we were generous with it.

For my health, my body was at its perfect weight and pain free. I got massages and acupuncture every month. I took the best supplements and had a regular walking, weight training, and Pilates routine. I expanded my self-love talk and spoke kindly to my body in the mirror.

My career was brilliant and evolved as I grew and changed. I saw myself as an international best-selling author. I was onstage sharing stories with other women and loving this new chapter of my life that led to new soul alliances, summits, books, and courses I would develop.

My mindset was my happiness key. It was my connection to my heart and soul, and spilled over into all aspects of my life. My contract with my COO was to practice positive self-talk with "I AM" statements and positive affirmations, and I agreed to meditate twice a day.

In the pages that follow, I'll share with you what some of my ninety-day soul contracts have looked like in the past:

A NINETY-DAY CONTRACT BETWEEN CEO AND CHO

I, Carrie Severson, declare love, light, and fun overflow in my life for the next ninety days. I give my love life over to my Chief Heart Officer to run with full responsibility.

My CHO calls in heart-centered men to have loving conversations and adventures with. I have heart-centered relationships show up on my path daily.

I agree to say yes to dates! I say yes to networking events and fun nights out with friends where I could potentially meet new people. I am easily introduced to new men who become friends and partners through my CHO. I agree to create a profile on dating websites, and my CHO attracts the right men to my life.

I go on two dates a month for the next ninety days and have the time of my life.

I have monthly meditation sessions with my CHO to talk about our progress and redirect as necessary.

My heart is full and alive. My CHO calls in my best friend and soul mate, and I trust my heart and CHO.

Signed,
Carrie Severson

A NINETY-DAY CONTRACT BETWEEN CEO AND COO

I, Carrie Severson, declare total peace and happiness in my life in the next ninety days. I rid my body of all that doesn't belong within it.

I give my COO total control over what steps to take in my body, soul, and mind alignment and recovery process.

I create positive I AM statements. I agree to practice longer meditations, go for walks regularly, and tell my family and friends when I'm stressed and need help.

New opportunities to meet people who are on the same path to overall peace and happiness come into my life easily.

My COO directs me on this path, and I listen and follow her lead. I receive messages I easily understand within my body and mind. I listen to my body and know when to lean back and rest. My COO and I have weekly meetings and redirect our weekly goals as necessary.

Signed,
Carrie Severson

A NINETY-DAY CONTRACT BETWEEN CEO AND CFO

I, Carrie Severson, declare new cash from my business will overflow in my life in the next ninety days and support me in ways that are beyond my wildest dreams. My Chief Financial Officer calls in soul-aligned clients from all around me.

My CFO and I have one meeting a week within these ninety days to discuss ways in which my CFO is attracting money and how I can show up to take action. We discuss bills that must be paid on time and organizations we'll give to with this new shower of cash.

I agree to connection calls that come my way, signing new clients that need support, and putting three offers of programs I can host out to the public.

With the new cash flow in my life, I buy healthy foods. I fulfill my self-care needs. I take myself out to networking events, take myself out on dates, and take classes that may lead to new friends and soul alliances.

My CFO provides me an opportunity to feel supported, secure, healthy, light, sexy, fulfilled, and heart centered.

I trust her to manifest and create financial stability in my life.

Signed,
Carrie Severson

A NINETY-DAY CONTRACT BETWEEN CEO AND CSO

I, Carrie Severson, declare myself as the CEO of the Unapologetic Voice House. I declare soul-aligned opportunities to further my career and purpose.

My Chief Story Officer brings forth new soul clients and soul alliances that provide me with joyful opportunities to earn a living, share my light, and provide direction to others who are looking for ways to share their stories.

I am filled up in all ways, thanks to my CSO, over the next ninety days and meet new parts of myself I haven't seen before as a way to lead authors I have yet to meet.

These opportunities connect me to soul-aligned people, and I have so much fun. I feel alive, aligned, and bright. I am supported in my career and serve it to the best of my ability.

My CSO and I have weekly meetings over the next ninety days. We discuss dreams, desires, possibilities, and opportunities to take action on. We spend time together in these meetings and focus on calling soul alliances that my CSO feels are best for me.

I trust and follow steps my CSO shows me. I take action, and these steps lead me to stages, clients, and partners and to feeling supportive, peaceful, and fun!

Signed,
Carrie Severson

A NINETY-DAY CONTRACT BETWEEN CEO AND CWBO

I, Carrie Severson, declare my Chief Well-Being Officer my best friend and right hand for the next ninety days. My CWBO is my sounding board as my CHO, COO, CFO, and CSO work their magic in their respective areas of my life.

My CWBO has a responsibility to me to help me stay aligned and on track for the next ninety days with these other four areas of my life. We meet weekly to go over my goals, dreams, and self-love practices, and the opportunities coming to me.

I trust my own heart and CWBO with every cell in my body.

I am taken care of, supported, secure, and happy. I am healthy, sexy, and a miracle worker in life.

Manifestations easily find their way into my life. I am a magnet for soul alliances and soul-aligned clients and opportunities.

And so it is.

Signed,
Carrie Severson

Now, below is some space to create your own soul contracts. Take some time to really feel out what these areas of your life could look like. What is it you welcome, desire, and are ready for in the love, health, money, career, and mindset areas of your life?

LOVE

1. _____

_____

_____

_____

2. _____

_____

_____

_____

3. _____

_____

_____

_____

HEALTH

1. _____

_____

_____

_____

2. _____

_____

_____

_____

3. _____

_____

_____

MONEY

1. _____

_____

_____

_____

2. _____

_____

_____

_____

3. _____

_____

_____

_____

CAREER

1. _____

_____

_____

_____

2. _____

_____

_____

_____

3. _____

_____

_____

_____

MINDSET

1. _____

_____

_____

_____

2. _____

_____

_____

_____

3. _____

_____

_____

_____

Appendix B
EXERCISES TO REDEFINE SELF-LOVE

S ELF-LOVE SOMETIMES FELT LIKE A BUZZWORD TO ME. IT FELT like a competition that I wasn't winning. It felt like I was doing self-love wrong because I never felt rejuvenated after something I thought was in the self-love bucket. Eventually, I assumed my peers were reading something I wasn't or watching something I wasn't.

There was shame involved in it.

I would see a post online from a woman living her best life in some beautiful home, in a bikini at a spa pool, or in some gorgeous setting with her friends or lover with something along the lines of "Filling up my cup" or "Work hard, play harder" or

"Sunday Funday" in the caption. I'd think, *Once I can do that, I'll feel better about my life. My stress will be gone.*

I'd keep scrolling on some social media platform and see images of a woman doing some intense yoga move in the desert, looking totally at peace. I'd think, *I like the kind of yoga where you just lie there with your feet up the wall for like twenty minutes. Maybe I should try doing that kind of yoga, and I'll find peace within.*

Images of spa treatments, manicures, new clothes, and jewelry—they all made me question my relationship with self-love and myself.

The concept of self-love started out as this thing I only did on the weekends, and it involved going places, spending money, and usually seeing someone else.

Before launching Severson Sisters, Saturdays were the days I would do an intense workout, go get my nails and toes done, go fill up on treats for myself, and sometimes go out, sometimes lie on the couch.

Sundays were days I went to church and had dinner with family or friends, and that was it.

All those things are totally acceptable self-love action items. But I still felt empty, like something was missing. And that's really why I never felt like I was doing the self-love thing right. Because I still felt a void in my life.

After Severson Sisters, there wasn't time or money for most of my weekend "treats" so the void just grew. Then came the fertility treatments and the breaking of my immune system. Self-love came to mean something else to me because all I had energy for was self-acceptance and self-reliance.

Napping was my self-love.

Daydreaming was self-love.

Letting myself cry was practicing self-love.

Sitting on a bench and pretending tree roots were coming out of my feet was my self-love practice.

Watching clouds roll by was how I filled my cup.

Walking on the beach and giving gratitude to the ocean was self-love.

Actively noticing the colors of the leaves around me was self-love.

The more I accepted my daily actions and inactions as self-love, the smaller that void in my life became. Until one day, that feeling was replaced with true love for myself.

Redefining Self-Love Exercise
One

UNPROGRAMMING
SELF-LOVE

RESHAPING HOW YOU THINK ABOUT SELF-LOVE IS SO important. You can go practice yoga upside down in the desert and be at total peace. That can be your act of self-love. But if it's not your thing, don't make it your thing.

This is your space and place to create your thing. Just for you. Nobody can live your life for you, so make sure you love it, live it out loud unapologetically, and enjoy it fully.

I love you.

STEP 1: DESCRIBING SELF-LOVE

In the space below, write down all the things you've learned about self-love and what it means.

_____

_____

_____

_____

_____

_____

_____

_____

_____

_____

_____

_____

_____

_____

STEP 2: ACTIONS AND FEELINGS

Now write down all the things you've done in the past for your own self-love practice.

_____

_____

_____

_____

_____

_____

_____

_____

_____

_____

_____

_____

_____

STEP 3: WITH FEELING NOW

Without using the word self-love, *write down as many words or phrases as you can to describe how self-love feels. Examples: sexy, free, honored, important, valuable, confident, bold.*

_____

_____

_____

_____

_____

_____

_____

_____

_____

_____

_____

_____

STEP 4: NARROW IT DOWN

Let's pinpoint three to five words from your list above. Write them down again in the space below and next to your word, write down actions you can do to induce those feelings. Examples: Valuable—When I speak up in a meeting and use my voice, I feel valuable. Free—When I ride my bike on an open road, I feel free. Sexy—I feel sexy when I smile and make eye contact with people.

1. _____

_____

_____

_____

2. _____

_____

_____

_____

3. _____

_____

_____

_____

Redefining Self-Love Exercise Two

YOUR FAVORITE PASTIMES

Y OUR SELF-LOVE PRACTICE DOESN'T HAVE TO LOOK LIKE anyone else's. And you don't have to prove it or justify it to anyone. That was hard for me. Sitting in meditation is an act of self-love. But so is exercising, napping, reading a book, crying, watching the clouds, taking a deep breath, and just looking at yourself in the mirror and smiling. You get to decide what self-love is to you.

Write down all the things you can do or already do that make you feel the adjectives you mentioned in the previous exercises. List whatever comes to mind.

_____

_____

_____

_____

_____

_____

_____

_____

_____

_____

_____

_____

_____

Redefining Self-Love Exercise Three

YOUR HIGHEST GOOD

THIS WAS PROBABLY THE HARDEST EXERCISE FOR MY OWN growth. Being able to recognize who I had to let go of from my day-to-day life for the sake of my mental health, well-being, and overall growth was not easy. I had created pockets of friends, acquaintances, and colleagues I could turn to. Instead, I decided to put energy into the people in my life I knew, without a doubt, wanted the best for me. I focused on them. I gave gratitude for them. And soon, my life started to shift. People who weren't helping me find my highest good started to create distance from me and me from them. It happened naturally.

STEP 1: ACKNOWLEDGING SUPPORT

Write down three to five individuals in your daily life who you know support your highest good. And then write down why you feel supported. Example: I feel supported by my boss. She goes out of her way to point out what I'm doing right in my job, and that lifts my spirits. Feeling witnessed for what I do makes me feel proud.

1. _____

   _____

   _____

2. _____

   _____

   _____

3. _____

   _____

   _____

STEP 2: ACKNOWLEDGING ACTIONS

Next, it's important to acknowledge your own actions. How do you respond in each of the scenarios you listed above? Do you support your highest good in each scenario? Example: When I feel supported by my boss, I come home feeling happier and have energy to go for a walk with the dog.

1. _____

_____

_____

_____

2. _____

_____

_____

_____

3. _____

_____

_____

_____

4. _____

_____

_____

_____

5. _____

_____

_____

_____

Redefining Self-Love Exercise
Four

I AM . . .

THESE TWO WORDS ARE POWERFUL. I FILLED MY JOURNALS with affirmations, mantras, and prayers that all started with the words *I AM.* They are important. What I found, though, is that at first, they were just words. I didn't recognize the power they held because I couldn't feel it. That is, until I started to connect feelings and actions to them. After a while of doing these exercises, I recognized a shift within.

STEP 1: YOU GOT THIS

Looking back at your answers to the questions in Appendix B, write out I AM statements about how you already practice self-love. Examples: I AM loving myself when I take the dog for a walk. I AM loving myself when I use my voice in meetings.

1. _____

   _____

   _____

   _____

2. _____

   _____

   _____

   _____

3. _____

   _____

   _____

   _____

4. _____

   _____

_____

_____

5. _____

_____

_____

_____

STEP 2: RESHAPING SELF-LOVE

Your idea of self-love can change each day. Nobody's doing this for you. It's all in your control. In this space, write down your definition of self-love in this moment. Examples: Right now, in this moment, self-love means finishing this book and putting it out into the world for women to connect with. To me, in this moment, self-love is an awareness that I completed something I spent eight years working on and doing a dance party in the living room with my husband to celebrate.

_____

_____

_____

_____

_____

_____

_____

_____

_____

_____

_____

_____

_____

_____

_____

_____

_____

_____

_____

_____

_____

Acknowledgments

U NAPOLOGETICALLY *ENOUGH* TOOK EIGHT YEARS TO WRITE. The number of people who impacted my life over the course of this creation can fill an entire book. In all honesty, I've thanked so many of you along the way that my hope is you already know what you mean to me.

Mom, you're amazing. Thank you for being with me for all these major milestones. Dad, you're my rock. Thank you for always providing me with a home and a way back to it whenever I needed it. To the original Severson sister, Holly, I am so grateful God made us family. Thank you for saying yes to all my big ideas and for being such a blessing to me.

Sean, Tara, Brad, and kids, thank you for adding such sweetness to my life.

Angie, what I've learned from you has helped me over and over again. I'm so grateful to you and what you bring to the world.

Eileen, I pray every woman has a woman like you in her circle. Thank you for being such an amazing friend. And to all my soul sisters who helped me find my voice while writing this book and read it before anyone else, your sisterhood is so important to me.

Danielle, I'll always remember where I was when I received your title advice. *Unapologetically Enough* has been a true gift. Thank you for your partnership.

Vanessa, thank you for creating this magical cover design.

Gavin, you are my favorite person. Our relationship is by far my most cherished soul quest. I love you. Thank you for loving and supporting me as wildly and as deeply as you do.

And finally, to the readers of *Unapologetically Enough*, I'd like to say thank you for reading this book. It means a lot to me. And so do you.

About the Author

CARRIE SEVERSON IS AN AUTHOR AND THE CHIEF EXECUTIVE Officer of her life and the Unapologetic Voice House, an independent book publishing business. She has been in the storytelling industry for nearly twenty-five years. She is an entrepreneur who started the Unapologetic Voice House in 2019 after spending five years pitching literary agents in the hopes of being published traditionally. All her rejection letters from literary agents came down to the same thing: They all loved the work. They all compared the work to well-known authors. But she didn't have a big enough platform for them to take her on as a client. So Carrie launched a company that could help women just like her, who were unapologetic in their stories and looking for support. She's married to her best friend and on her next soul quest to become the next version of herself. She hopes you enjoyed this book and find her on social media platforms listed below or various websites she runs to share your thoughts: UnapologeticallyEnough.com and TheUnapologeticVoiceHouse.com.

Facebook.com/carrieseverson.storyteller
Instagram.com/the_unapologetic_voice_house
Linkedin.com/feed/carrie_severson